SCANDINAVIAN STYLE

BRADLEY QUINN

SPECIAL PHOTOGRAPHY BY **ALEXANDER CRISPIN**
STYLING BY KELLY RUSSELL

FOR INGELA

Published in 2003 by Conran Octopus Limited
a part of the Octopus Publishing Group
2–4 Heron Quays, London E14 4JP
www.conran-octopus.co.uk

British Library Cataloguing-in-Publication Data. A catalogue record
for this book is available from the British Library.

ISBN 1 84091 325 8

Printed in China

Publishing Director: Lorraine Dickey
Art Director: Chi Lam
Art Editor: Megan Smith
Executive Editor: Zia Mattocks
Editor: Alison Wormleighton
Picture Research Manager: Liz Boyd
Picture Researcher: Sarah Hopper
Map Illustrator: Russell Bell
Production Manager: Angela Couchman

CONTENTS

INTRODUCTION The beauty of nature has exerted a strong influence over the decorative styles of the Scandinavian countries for many centuries. Design traditions have long been characterized by a wide range of visual symbols and organic forms that directly reflect the enjoyment of the beautiful Nordic landscape.

ABOVE *For centuries, influences from the natural world have shaped the design traditions of the Nordic countries and continue to be a defining characteristic today.*

RIGHT *The soft glow of candlelight warms the Scandinavian home. The subtle colours, soft textures and simple motifs of traditional textiles complement the rustic wood patinas of cherished antiques to create a cosy, inviting atmosphere.*

The lands of the far north, as points on a compass, lie in a clear direction, but their cultural geography is less fixed. Historically, the Nordic region was believed to be farthest away from the civilized societies of the south, and for most of its long history it was isolated from the Near East and the Mediterranean. From Mesopotamia and Egypt, civilization spread to Greece, Rome and Crete, and tales of the barbarians who nestled on the northern outskirts of Europe made their way of life seem primitive and remote. The myths of savage Norsemen persisted well into the Middle Ages, when marauding Viking warriors terrorized their southerly neighbours. Yet, even as the Vikings plundered the treasures of Europe, they also gained a reputation for being a cultured and learned people. The Norsemen were exquisite craftsmen and intrepid explorers whose seafaring skills brought them to North America some five hundred years before Columbus.

Throughout time, knowledge of the Nordic cultures has been obscured by geographical distance and the perception of a landscape perpetually steeped in winter. While the roots of the word 'south' are linked to 'sun', the etymology of 'north' is less salubrious. The term was linked to 'night' and to 'darkness', and to the seven stars of Ursa Major visible in the northern sky. According to the ancient Greeks, the distant lands of the far north lay directly beneath these stars, stretching from the northern shores of the Black Sea to the region above the Alps. The medieval Germans and Dutch thought of the north as the coastal regions strung along the Baltic: territories occupied by the Danes, the Poles and the Russians. The Danes themselves referred to Sweden and Norway as the north, while the inhabitants of Sweden regarded Swedish Lapland as the northern frontier. To the Laplanders, the north was the northernmost Norwegian province of Finnmark, whose inhabitants considered the north to be the Arctic icecap beyond the islands of the Barents Sea.

Their geography still shapes outsiders' perception of the character of the Nordic countries. To them, the far north appears to be a cold, dark, mysterious region tempered by extreme summer light and enveloped in a mood of melancholy and solitude. Dramatic fjords and dense forests come to mind, contrasted with rugged plains and broad horizons. But in the collective imagination of the Nordic peoples, nature represents a powerful reality that has exerted a strong influence over their decorative traditions for centuries.

While the Nordic nations are united by their reverence for the natural world and their ability to overcome the hardships of the harsh climate, the boundaries between them are

defined by the landscape. Sweden and Finland, with their networks of deep lakes, rocky islands and vast forests, suggest the dawning of creation, when water and earth first separated, with many of these two countries' landscapes continuing to reflect their prehistoric separation from the seabed. As the temperate waters of the Gulf Stream churn through the North Sea, its warm currents make these northern climates more temperate than those in latitudes farther to the east, which are characterized by a near-perpetual winter. The Gulf Stream warms Denmark's meandering hills and dales, and flows past Norway's breathtaking coastline before turning towards Iceland.

With its volcanoes and dramatic, windswept moors, Iceland's volatile terrain has a completely different atmosphere from the other Nordic landscapes. There are no forests, only a few stunted trees, but the lava fields, hot springs, vast glaciers and beaches of black sand create a landscape unlike anywhere else on earth.

Despite their close geographic proximity, the mainland Nordic nations have always been markedly distinct from each other. The historical idea of Scandinavia as a single entity with a shared culture is a source of astonishment – and often amusement – to the Nordic peoples today. Although Norway, Sweden, Finland and Denmark boast a similar type of lifestyle, and Norwegian, Swedish and Danish stem from the same linguistic family (to speak one language is to understand the others), the differences between them are as distinct as those that differentiate other European nations from each other. In terms of design, the aesthetic principles of minimalism, clarity, understated stylistic features and naturalistic beauty are generally present in most of the Nordic decorative traditions, but the treatment of materials and the artistic élan vary widely from country to country.

The five Nordic countries are members of *Nordiska Rådet*, the Nordic council that addresses cultural and political issues that impact on the region. Norway, Denmark and Sweden evolved from a common Viking heritage which gradually disintegrated into warring kingdoms, and the boundaries between them were disputed for many centuries. As modern-day states, these countries retain strong national identities while acknowledging that the historical and linguistic legacies of their forebears originated from an ancient 'Scandinavian' culture. Iceland was populated by Vikings from Norway in the ninth century; and, although its linguistic origins, religious orientation and family names clearly relate to the mainland, the Icelandic language is generally incomprehensible to those living in Scandinavia today, and its cultural traditions are equally unique.

Culturally and linguistically, Finland is said to be closer to the East than to the Scandinavian cultures. The Finnish language is thought to have originated in the Ural Mountains, belonging to the Ugric family of languages spoken in Hungary and Estonia today. For several centuries, Finland was annexed to Sweden and Swedish was stipulated as the official language. Finland became an autonomous Grand Duchy of Russia in 1809 before gaining its independence early in the twentieth century. Many of the colonial Swedes chose to stay in Finland, and subsequent generations remained true to their Swedish heritage, creating a parallel Finnish-Swedish culture that today identifies more with Sweden, Norway and Denmark than with the other Baltic nations.

While the Finns can sometimes come across as serious and reserved, they feel that their temperament has more in common with the fiery angst of the Russians than with the subdued rationality of the stereotypical Scandinavian persona. Their design sensibilities stir dark passions – the colours of the early Marimekko textiles captured something very primal, and the elegant designs of Eliel Saarinen and Alvar Aalto were poetic expressions of materials and form. Norway is an energetic, sporty nation, and its inhabitants have a characteristically cheerful vitality and a friendly, unpretentious manner. Swedes think of themselves as sophisticated, objective and self-assured, exuding a confidence that can sometimes be mistaken for arrogance. The Icelandics are equally self-confident, eager to take charge and reluctant to declare any task complete before perfection has been meticulously exacted. Denmark is a land of exuberance, a country where fantasy and imagination shape and engender a laid-back approach among its inhabitants, as well as the modernist dynamics of the designers Arne Jacobsen, Finn Juhl and Verner Panton.

LEFT *A disciple of Alvar Aalto, Marjatta Brummer worked as an architect in Helsinki before establishing a practice in Stockholm. Her own house, which she designed and built in the early 1960s, drew upon Aalto's characteristic treatment of light, volume and proportion. The living room windows are especially large in scale, bringing nature indoors and making the house feel closer to the waterfront.*

Each Nordic country played a significant role in the formation of modernism, contributing to the birth of modern style with streamlined, sculptural designs that were as functional as they were beautiful. The Nordic nations were the first to accept social equality, industrialization and urbanization as tenets of modern life, yet they remained true to the individual legacies of craftsmanship that had for centuries given a specific identity to each design tradition. As with most of Europe, modern design in Scandinavia effected a dynamic shift from provincial isolation to national self-promotion as a European platform for design began to take shape. By the mid-twentieth century, however, the Nordic countries' distinctive design vocabularies had become known internationally as 'Scandinavian', usually without reference to individual nationalities. So-called 'Scandinavian' designs appeared to be unified by their understated elegance, high-quality craftsmanship and natural materials, and were recognized internationally as a non-elitist, minimal style that remained within reach of the everyday householder.

The concept of Scandinavian style represented in this book moves away from the premise that the decorative traditions of the Nordic nations should be interpreted as a common aesthetic or as a single design signature. Instead, *Scandinavian Style* explores what an individualistic approach can reveal about the architecture, interior design, furniture craftsmanship, decorative arts and textile traditions that characterize the far north, as well as the inspirations driving the individual Nordic designers and their distinctive craftsmanship.

Throughout the last century, modern Scandinavian designers produced compelling works that have been acclaimed as design classics. A large number have remained in continuous production since they were designed, and many still provide a source of inspiration to the new generation of Nordic designers. The timelessness of these designs indicates that the 'Scandinavian' style is not just a fleeting moment of design history, but a tradition that will continue long into the future.

Scandinavian Style explores the rich traditions that shape Nordic interiors in a quest to uncover the elements that have created its timeless style. Combining its distinctive forms of furniture design, ceramics, glass-ware and textiles with the role of architecture and the impact of lighting, the book details the beauty of antiques, time-honoured craftsmanship and decorative arts, revealing the value of traditional colours, motifs and natural materials. As a practical guide to introducing a lighter, more streamlined style into the home, it presents a fresh vision for the modern living space and a new approach to the traditional interior. *Scandinavian Style* will have a strong appeal to anyone with an appreciation of pure form, design innovation, understated luxury and timeless elegance.

THIS PAGE *The contemporary Scandinavian home is often characterized by a reverence for classical elements and a visionary approach to maximizing space. Here, a pair of Poul Kjærholm chairs sit atop a Kasthall rug based on a design by Thomas Eriksson. The low pine table by Shideh Shaygan transforms planes of wood into an elegant centrepiece.*

**ARCHITECTURE
& TRADITION**

ARCHITECTURE & TRADITION An almost minimal approach to space gives Nordic architecture a subdued elegance. Each architectural style introduced a new vision of living, linking furniture and interior design with the house. Many styles remain contemporary today, as architects revive details of past eras.

ABOVE *For centuries, deal floors and low ceilings have formed the basis for the country* stuga, *or cottage. This one was updated with a 'modern'* kakelugn *(ceramic stove) from the early 1900s.*
RIGHT *Wall borders and wainscoting decorate this late-Gustavian interior. The simplicity of the architecture was reflected in the furniture of the period, as this 1810 couch illustrates.*

Strongly rooted in the natural world, the houses of the far north seem to belong to nature's kingdom more than to the cultivated environments of man. The dwellings built amid the labyrinths of dense forests, cavernous lakes and broad riverbanks of the Scandinavian regions were never conceived as artificial environments, but as a means of living in harmony with the volatile forces of nature.

While the Nordic landscape shaped patterns of habitation and engendered characteristic robustness in those who could endure its extremes, it also nurtured their survival. Rough beams of heavy pine timber, long ribbons of birch bark, granite deposits and wedges of turf have provided homes for the Nordic peoples for thousands of years, protecting them against one of the harshest climates on earth.

Despite its severe winter temperatures, Scandinavia – Norway, Finland, Denmark, Sweden and Iceland – is a landscape of intense beauty. In the high northern latitudes, the sun bathes the landscape with light, colouring the sky with luminous shades of dark purple, deep blue and subtle crimson. The Scandinavian landscape comes alive during the long summer days and light nights of the midnight sun, and then becomes majestically silent as the autumn colours fade into the white snowfalls of winter.

Water is ever-present. An unbroken chain of islands flanks the long Baltic coastline of Sweden and Finland, and 50,000 islands trace the dramatic rock face of Norway's Atlantic shore. Norway's and Iceland's coastlines are indented with innumerable fjords, while lakes, rivers and streams abound in the Norwegian, Swedish and Finnish landscapes.

The sea has often been the clearest demarcation of Scandinavia's frontiers, as the boundaries between the Nordic territories remained in flux for several millennia. The earliest houses were not built according to territorial or national styles, but were determined simply by the accessibility of the materials around them and the protection afforded by the landscape. Along the coast, low dwellings were sheltered from the wind by high boulders and rocky crags, their foundations dug into pits of earth in order to draw their shape as flat as possible against the land. Upright buildings were built among groves of pine or fir trees, whose branches formed a natural outer barrier that provided protection from the winds and shelter from the cold. Though primitive, these early Nordic homes were much more than mere refuges from harsh weather. Their cosy intimacy brought together the fostering spirit of nature and the nesting instincts of man.

Viking legacies

The Vikings are best known for their piracy and plundering, but on their own territory life was peaceful and well ordered. Homesteads were built among inland lakes and fjords in settlements consisting of one or two main farms. Called 'longhouses' because of their lateral shapes and low, windowless walls, the Vikings' houses were typically constructed of canework panels stretched across a timber framework and coated with thick mire. Oiled animal skins were stretched across wall openings near the eaves. Known as 'wind's-eyes', the thin skins enabled a small amount of light to pass through while averting the blowing wind.

The roof of the longhouse was cut from the earth around it. Rolls of turf were excised from the soil and joined together in a layer of living thatch that made the house almost indistinguishable from the landscape. Timber was not easy to harvest or work with at that time, and only the most prosperous Viking chieftains had the means of building great log houses of several rooms. As the timber shafts were stacked laterally to form the walls, the wide crevices between them were plugged with moss or turf and caulked with clay.

The centre of the Viking home was dominated by a wide hearth, open on all sides so as to radiate heat and light in every direction. A low beam was fixed crosswise astride the hearth, extending from wall to wall, to furnish a support from which iron cooking pots could hang. Torches or oil lamps supplied other sources of light, placed beneath vents cut into the rooftop to allow the smoke to escape. Furniture was scant – benches or low platforms were built into the sloping walls to provide seating during the day and beds at night. Storerooms and workshops usually occupied the shallow cellars known as 'pit houses' dug alongside the main house. A sloping roof was built to shield the goods inside from foraging animals and the forces of nature.

When more space was needed, additional buildings were erected; storerooms, workshops, barns, saunas and guest huts were clustered around the main house. The isolation of remote farmsteads necessitated considerable stores to sustain the family throughout winter, with storehouses substantial enough to house them. Domestic space was seldom confined to a single building, but interspersed among several structures, and such simple, utilitarian buildings framed everyday human activities. These homes differed from those built in the Mediterranean at this time, in which the rooms were centred around an open courtyard where domestic tasks were performed in the warmth of the sun.

The homes of the Viking period began to take the form we recognize in the modern day as Christianity gained ground in Scandinavia around AD1000. Christianity introduced an essentially Roman treatment of living space and gradually infused the Viking culture with decorative and architectural influences from England, France, Germany and Italy. The Romanesque style had spread to Scandinavia from Germany and Lombardy, but also from Byzantium in the East. Eastern influences were nothing new to the Nordic peoples; Viking runic inscriptions often reference Byzantium and the Eastern lands south of the Caspian Sea.

The longhouses of the Vikings gave way to the intimate confines of snug cabins as the Romanesque period evolved. Known as *stugor*, these rustic cabins divided domestic space into separate areas, generally small rooms that could be heated effectively against the winter cold. These simple homes were Romanesque in their treatment of space but not in their architectural features, as their walls were built in a Nordic style with squared logs that were secured with dovetail joints. While the interior of a *stuga* was divided into several small rooms, the ceilings remained low and timber still prevailed as the principal building material. The main hearth was situated in a central, multi-purpose room where food was prepared and domestic tasks carried out. The thick outside walls of a *stuga* were covered simply with pine staves, leaving the supporting beams overhead in full view. Hanging textiles lined the walls of affluent homes and enfolded sleeping spaces to provide additional warmth.

The Romanesque style found full expression in houses built from stone, emphasizing the sculpture and architectural styles from other parts of Europe. Fortified castles and large manor houses were built in a distinctively continental style. In these grand homes, traditional architectural details took on a stylistic vocabulary, and by the twelfth and early thirteenth centuries few Viking influences remained. Quarried stone was left uncut to form dense walls of up to one metre (three feet) in depth that supported the heavy vaulted roofs. This created a solid architectural framework that was, for the most part, fire-resistant. Window openings were small and placed near the ceiling, and the rough walls beneath them were rarely decorated by the frescoes common to Mediterranean homes at the time.

The Romanesque style that unfolded in Norway and Denmark did, however, incorporate vestiges of Viking folklore and mythology into its decorative detailing. The images of the mythological gods were crafted into blocks of stone cut for house-building and placed near the eaves, windows and doorways. Similarly, wooden posts and timber supports also featured the fierce expressions of pagan deities. Although the peoples of the Nordic lands had converted to Christianity several hundred years earlier, they still relied upon the Viking gods to guard and protect their homes for many centuries.

FAR LEFT AND LEFT *The Vikings travelled far and wide, bringing a range of architectural and stylistic influences back to their homeland. The Vikings' tools were among the most advanced in Europe and were used to craft fine furniture, figurative works and exquisitely carved architectural details. Their ships were conceived as floating architecture, and were much more technically advanced than the homes the Vikings designed. The towering prow and sternpost of a Viking ship were eventually replicated on dry land in the form of Norway's medieval stave architecture, which was richly decorated with mythological figures and abstract linear patterns. Several of these stave buildings from the eleventh and twelfth centuries were beautifully restored during the twentieth century, preserving the last relics of Viking architecture.*

The Nordic *stuga*

The Viking method of building houses out of soil, wood and uncut stone continued until the late nineteenth century in Scandinavian regions where timber was scarce. In Iceland, where the absence of forests meant that most building materials would have to be dug from the earth, building with turf and uncut stone persisted out of necessity for hundreds of years. On the mainland, however, most regions of Scandinavia had abundant resources of timber, and the legacy of Viking craftsmanship made it possible to construct relatively sophisticated dwellings using only simple tools.

From medieval times, the main room of the *stuga* was arranged according to a diagonal plan. Moved from the *stuga's* centre, the fireplace was built into the corner and encircled by stone, with the hearth raised nearly to waist level so that cooking could be done more comfortably. The smoke was drawn upwards through a chimney rather than being funnelled through an opening in the rooftop as it had been in the Viking longhouses. This style of house was widely built in the seventeenth-century American colony of New Sweden, located in present-day Delaware. Even after the Swedish withdrew from North America, these timber houses remained popular among the other colonists, who continued to build log cabins in the style as they moved westwards to settle the land.

In Sweden, Finland and Norway, the simple log *stuga* was clad with sawn timber to create a more refined facade as sawn boards became available. In Denmark, large farmhouses evolved according to the materials at hand, creating a different architectural style altogether. Lacking the vast forests of the countries across the Baltic, the Danes made their supply of timber go farther by using a half-timbering technique. A timber framework was constructed according to a system of square modules that were filled in with mud and twigs. The timber framework was left exposed and stained with tar, while the filled spaces in between were whitewashed. Surviving examples can be found in the southern Swedish provinces of Skåne and Blekinge, which were Danish domains until the mid-seventeenth century.

Bedrooms were seldom determined by the original layout of the *stuga's* structure, but constructed as cupboards once the *stuga* was finished. The bed frames were usually attached to the walls on one side, with supporting posts fitted from floor to ceiling on the other. The frames were most often encircled by wooden panels, with a curtained opening for access left on one side. Alternatively, bed frames could be enclosed by hanging textiles, animal hides or furs rather than wood. Depending on the skills of the men of the household or the availability of local carpenters, these early bed frames might also incorporate shelving and storage or add an ornately carved feature to the rooms where they were built.

By the eighteenth century, the *stuga* had expanded to comprise a vestibule, a multi-purpose room dominated by the household's hearth and several other rooms that opened off the vestibule or the main room itself. Small, leaded glass windows allowed in more natural light, while whitewashed walls and roof beams gave the interior a brighter feel. Doors and door frames featured modest architraves or carved relief. Furniture was commonly built into the walls, and long benches were constructed beside the dining table to provide practical seating and storage. Cupboards, corner cabinets and shelves were also built directly into the timber walls and were seen as part of the architecture.

ABOVE *Ancient timber buildings evolved into the stuga, the architectural standard of the Nordic countryside. This stuga was built on Matsgården farm in the Swedish province of Dalarna in the nineteenth century, and was furnished in a style that had remained relatively the same for three centuries. Carved wood was used to shape and define the features and function of each room, with most items of furniture built directly into the interior architecture. The grandfather clock was built into the bedstead.*

Period elegance

From the dramatic arches of the Gothic period to the elegant designs of the rococo style, Nordic house-builders maintained a long tradition of importing architectural elements from abroad and reinterpreting them with local materials and Nordic tastes. The architecture that resulted combined a diverse range of 'new' building techniques, structural supports and ornamental facades with the same colours and masonry finishes that had been used in Scandinavia for several centuries.

As the architectural styles changed over the centuries, they reflected the growth in commerce that occurred as Nordic merchants strengthened trade with other countries and boosted the prosperity of the region. With local architects gaining more technical expertise from abroad, enabling them to design more extravagant styles for the city dignitaries and landed gentry, town houses became taller and country manor houses expanded laterally. A surprising number of these homes survive today, and their architecture provides a visual record of changes in living standards and lifestyle habits through the centuries. Many Scandinavian architects continue to find inspiration in these period styles.

Gothic architecture

As Romanesque style gave way to Gothic at the approach of the fourteenth century, the architectural ingenuity and exquisite workmanship the new style fostered enabled craftsmen to build higher walls and steeper roofs, streamlining their masonry finishes and refining the style of timber buildings. Stone houses became larger and more sophisticated, with the pointed Gothic arch providing greater structural support than the round Romanesque arches had, and producing new stylistic elements. The Gothic home was brighter and more spacious than its Romanesque predecessor, and the tradition of building in timber and stone was supplemented by the imported skill of working with brick. Gothic stylistic details introduced Nordic craftsmen to the styles of central and southern Europe, and they imitated them in their own interiors. Wood was substituted for stone, elaborate ornamentation was replaced by subtle detailing, and walls were smoothed and painted to resemble fine relief or carved decoration. Neither bricks nor stones were moulded into uniform shapes, and as a result the finished walls had a characteristic irregular texture.

Germanic influences

The Hanseatic towns established by German burghers in the thirteenth and fourteenth centuries contain some of Scandinavia's best examples of medieval architecture. Houses in Visby, Bergen, Ålborg and Turku were influenced by the culture of urban living introduced by émigrés from German towns and cities. As German merchants settled towns in the Baltic region and along Norway's Atlantic coast, they continued to build in the distinctive architectural styles of the Rhineland and Westphalia. Houses constructed in the stone masonry styles popular among German craftsmen from Saxony were built not only within the city walls but also in the countryside beyond them.

City houses were often a combination of commerce and dwelling, their layout oriented towards both receiving visitors and facilitating business transactions. The house typically included storerooms or guest accommodation alongside the family's own rooms. Urban homes commonly had a jettied upper storey cantilevered over the street below, surmounted by gabled roofs on the street side. In the rural towns, where wood was the primary material, overhanging upper floors were the norm in large houses. In the Bergslagen region of Sweden, the medieval *svalgångshus*, or gallery house, was widespread. The *svalgångshus* featured an open gallery on the upper floors that gave access to storerooms, to the bedrooms of an inn, or to separate apartments on the floors above.

Scandinavian and German elements came together again several centuries later, when Scandinavian architects worked in Germanic regions during the seventeenth century. Ornamental Nordic styles were expressed in the domestic architecture of Swedish Pomerania, where Swedish officials built castles and manor houses in the classical baroque proportions common in Sweden at that time. Some were built with limestone imported from Gotland, with facades painted in the deep brownish-red tones of Falun red, an intense iron-oxide red.

Karolinskt houses

With the Reformation, in the early sixteenth century, architecture and craft traditions were influenced by the European Renaissance. However, Lutheran Protestantism did not express itself in magnificent temples, nor did it promote opulence in the interior. In the Nordic countries, the Reformation deprived the Roman Catholic Church of much of its power and wealth, and the building of churches and vicarages ground to a standstill. Whereas architects had previously been employed by the Church or appointed to the court, many turned to the merchant classes and prominent landowners for commissions.

From the mid-seventeenth to about the mid-eighteenth century, many country houses in Denmark, Finland and Sweden were built in the architecture of the baroque. In Sweden, a popular baroque style characterized the reigns of Karl X Gustav, Karl XI and Karl XII, who ruled in succession. Named *Karolinska* for the epoch, the style resembled England's Palladian architecture but was more austere in its decoration.

The classical elegance of *Karolinskt* manor houses commanded a strict rhythm of symmetry and uniformity. The house was built in wood, panelled with upright timber and decorated by pilaster strips (vertical strips of wood extending from the foundations to the roof), which capped the corners and divided the facade into separate window bays. Falun red coated the facade, rendering a strong contrast to the whitewashed woodwork. Usually the walls were topped by a *säteri* roof, the Scandinavian forerunner to the mansard roof. Its slope was interrupted by a narrow vertical wall perforated by tiny windows, the wall itself surmounted by a separate sloping rooftop.

The front doorway was the house's geometric centre, balanced by an equal number of windows on either side or flanked by wings of identical proportions. The main rooms were usually placed on either side of a vestibule which also provided access to the other rooms of the house, including a *långkammare* (literally 'long chamber'). Its elongated shape and doorways into adjoining rooms suggested a wide corridor in which the communal activities of the extended household could take place. *Karolinskt* homes had series of interconnecting square rooms, usually accessed by more than one doorway, but over time a long corridor spanning the length of the house became the norm, giving individuals greater privacy.

ABOVE *In Scandinavia, the rococo period was far simpler in expression than in the rest of Europe. The paintings of Johan Pasch, originally commissioned for the manor house at Läckö in 1753 and later moved to the billiard room at Åkerö, pictured here, exemplify the restraint that distinguished the style from its French counterpart. The walls show a typical illusionist technique but their illustrations were intended to give the impression of a room in use.*

Rococo and neoclassical styles

The Francophile orientation of eighteenth-century Scandinavian architects led to a wealth of palaces and manor houses being built throughout the region. The opulent rococo style that began in France in the early years of the eighteenth century was introduced to Sweden by Jean Eric Rehn, a designer, and Carl Hårleman, an architect appointed to the royal court. The Svartsjö Palace, near Stockholm, which Hårleman designed for Fredrik I and which was completed in 1739, was the first example of a rococo building in Sweden. In Denmark, the architect Nicolai Eigtved built the sweeping rococo pavilions at the Amalienborg Palace in Copenhagen, which became a major influence on the rococo style in Denmark.

As the rococo unfolded in Sweden, it was less ornate than its French counterpart, and was constructed in local materials rather than in the exquisite sandstone masonry used in France. Swedish rococo houses typically had facades of pale yellow plaster that imitated the honey-coloured sandstone prevalent in France. Hårleman's designs were characterized by strict symmetry and topped by mansard roofs. (Although this type of roof provided, in effect, an extra floor, this was used only as an attic, not as living space.) Rococo style also dominated the interiors of the royal palaces and grand houses built in Scandinavia during this time, but there was less surface carving and fewer textiles than in French rococo. Hårleman imported workmen from France to decorate the interior of the royal palace in Stockholm in a rococo style that bears a distinct Nordic signature.

Many of Hårleman's rococo buildings remain standing today. Åkerö, an exquisite mansion built on a private island in the inland lake Yngaren, is the most lavish of Hårleman's manor houses. The house was structured according to French architectural conventions, raising the ground-floor ceilings far higher than those of the floor above. The ground-floor windows were larger in scale than those on the upper floor and were separated by a band of masonry trim painted red to contrast with the pale yellow facade.

In 1752, Hårleman built the two-storey Granhammar manor house, which was more modest in its design but was no less influential in its style. Like Åkerö, Granhammar has a rendered stone facade and a mansard roof of painted sheet metal and terracotta tiles. Granhammar's floor plan was rectangular, with the main *salle* – the principal reception room – slightly offset from the centre of the otherwise symmetrical axis.

In 1755, the Swedish designer Carl Wijnblad published an influential book, *Architectural Drawings for Forty Domestic Houses of Stone and Thirty of Wood*, to spread the rococo style to the provinces beyond the capital. Wijnblad's publication featured elements of Hårleman's work along with rococo designs created by other Scandinavian architects and European craftsmen. The book included a stylistic vocabulary for a variety of houses, ranging from small log *stugor* to grand stone palaces. As a result, the pale yellow and cream colours used to decorate the facades of stone houses began to appear on wooden buildings, whose rustic horizontal timbers were clad in board architecture (vertical strips of wood).

By the second half of the eighteenth century, the rococo style was giving way to neoclassical influences, which persisted into the first half of the next century. In Denmark and Sweden, imposing country villas were based on the classical temple, introducing a distinctively European style of architecture beyond the cities and into the Nordic landscape.

Revival styles

The architecture of the second half of the nineteenth century was characterized by the popularity of Romantic revival styles such as Gothic, Renaissance, neo-baroque, pseudo-rococo and the 'Dragon' styles of the Viking era and the Middle Ages. Throughout the Scandinavian capitals, neo-Renaissance town houses were built in stone, while the board architecture continued to be the mainstay of country villas.

In Norway, the revival of old-fashioned timber styles represented a return to nationalistic roots. Eager to gain independence from Sweden, architects and craftsmen mined Norway's Viking heritage to establish a distinctive cultural identity. Timber villas were clad in wood panelling and embellished with motifs inspired by Viking ornamentation. The style was a hybrid of techniques taken from the construction of Viking ships and from the stave facades of Norway's ancient *stugor*. Mythological animal heads and long-necked dragons – ancient symbols for warding off evil – were carved on roof peaks, support brackets and balustrades, hence the name 'Dragon style'.

At this time, Norwegian architects also developed a distinctive type of wooden villa described as 'Swiss style'. Although Norway and Switzerland share a similar alpine terrain, the houses were not intended to imitate Swiss architecture. The style was a pastiche of vernacular timber construction, ornamental gables, and overhanging verandas traced through previous centuries of Norwegian architecture, and also included elements of 'Dragon style'. Incorporating exposed beams, jigsaw cut-outs and stylized columns, the villas featured some of the most elaborate facades ever built in Scandinavian architecture. Bay windows, woodwork balconies and carved brackets incorporated a range of curvaceous shapes and angular points. The roofs were often surmounted with ornamental ridges that ended in open-mouthed dragon heads that breathed forked-tongued fire over gable apexes. The Swiss style paralleled the 'Gingerbread' or 'Carpenter's Gothic' styles that flourished in the United States at the time – which did not benefit from the magical protection of the dragon.

Grand villas built in revival styles in Finland and Sweden were constructed according to classic architectural principles. Two- and three-storey houses were built to rules of strict symmetrical composition, creating a unified rectilinear layout that established a sense of balance throughout. Recalling the equilibrium expressed in *Karolinskt* houses, the main part of the house was flanked by single-storey wings on either side, with a projecting frontispiece or a peak-roofed porch framing the doorway. The villa's roofs were steep and Gothic; surmounted by pointed gables, they revived a particular style that had been common in medieval European houses. Wide eaves projected more than a metre (several feet) beyond the walls, providing additional protection against torrents of rain, snow and hailstones. The wooden facades might be tar-oiled in the style of traditional Norse *stugor* or painted in Falun red with whitewashed trim.

The Norwegian town of Ålesund, which was destroyed by fire in 1904, was rebuilt in a vernacular version of art nouveau architecture, as a miniature metropolis with broad avenues and scenic squares. Ålesund's new houses featured art nouveau facades flanked by towers and turrets imbued with stylistic expressions of romantic Norse mythology.

RIGHT *As the National Romantic movement took hold in Nordic architecture, local materials were chosen to represent the affinity between the nation and the landscape. Constructed from wide timber beams set atop a foundation of granite, Eliel Saarinen's home, Hvitträsk, shown here, represented the architectural revival as well as being an expression of nationalism.*

Romanticism and classicism

The late nineteenth century was characterized by a stylistic eclecticism. Swedish architects determined to embody Swedishness in architecture, much as the Norwegians had done with their own revival styles. A new generation of architects looked into the visual past and rediscovered neglected vernacular styles and craft traditions abundant in their heritage. The architectural style that Swedes now describe as National Romanticism was based on structural details from medieval fortresses and the timber dwellings of the landscape, combined with elements from the castles and manor houses of the baroque and rococo periods, plus influences from the Arts and Crafts movement of the late nineteenth century.

Houses built in the National Romantic style feature looming towers, spiralling turrets and curving balconies set within asymmetrical facades, whose thick walls give way to wide doorways and imposing window frames. Cut stone, heavy brickwork and wood trim articulate the houses' structural elements, while smooth stucco finishes give an impression of subdued refinement. Heavy timber styles also prevailed at the time, and a number of landmark wooden homes, such as the romantic villas by Lars Israël Wahlman, were built across the country.

The revival of timber styles spread to Finland, where the architect Eliel Saarinen built Hvitträsk, his own country home, from granite and timber. Indigenous to Finland, these styles became symbols of national identity during the Finnish National Romantic movement.

In the first two decades of the twentieth century, Swedish architects abandoned the strictly authentic articulation of classicism, and Nordic Classicism was born, interpreting the classical inheritance with a light-heartedness more akin to the buildings of southern Europe.

Nordic Classicism bypassed the bulky structures and heavy facades that typified houses of the National Romantic period, unfolding in the subtle elegance of Ionic columns, dentil mouldings, lunette windows, temple fronts, Grecian friezes and smooth plaster finishes. In Sweden, the style culminated in the elegant designs of Erik Gunnar Asplund, one of the country's foremost neoclassicist architects. The residential architecture he built in the style ranged from grand villas to small houses, and apartment buildings that varied in size and character. Asplund's playfully irreverent classicism, known internationally as Swedish Grace, attracted renewed interest during the postmodernism of the 1980s.

The rich and romantic history of Scandinavian architecture reveals a strong relationship to the styles and ideals of Europe, though sometimes pulling against them in a search for national identities. Irrespective of changes in tastes and styles, Scandinavian architecture maintains an unbroken tradition of bringing nature into architecture, so as architects looked towards new concepts of modern dwellings, their ideals continued to unfold through the use of natural materials and the timeless timber traditions expressed in previous centuries.

Functionalism

Scandinavian architecture came into its own during the modernist era. After the First World War, industrial and economic restructuring led to the rationalization of space and, consequently, the demand for simpler and more efficient styles of housing. The functionalistic, or *Funkis*, movement took hold in Stockholm and Oslo before spreading to the other Nordic cities. *Funkis* turned away from the nationalistic styles that had typified Scandinavia for nearly half a century, aligning the north with a growing international movement.

Although the modernist precepts of clarity, simplicity and exactness revolutionized the design traditions of continental Europe and North America, such principles had for a long time been defining features of Nordic architecture. The Nordic countries embraced modernism wholeheartedly, imbuing it with a revolutionary social thrust. The liberation of man and the role of architecture became firmly intertwined, and in Scandinavia the two have not been separated since. Modernism was not merely a style but also a system of living, evident in the tightly woven spatial connections – visual links – between architecture, interior design, furniture and household objects. Nordic architects advocated a philosophy of living that interpreted the house, the interior and the quality of life it sustained as a single spatial gesture.

Functionalism was virtually an official ideology in Sweden, where the establishment quickly embraced it as the means to remedy a growing housing shortage. Functionalist architecture became a metaphor for social policy and urbanization. As political leaders assimilated the belief that aesthetics could change people, the home became an instrument for shaping society itself. Outside of Sweden, the Danish and Norwegian authorities also responded to the practical solutions and simple economics advocated by the style, adopting the *Funkis* vision for urban modernism. *Funkis* developed into a uniquely Scandinavian brand of modernism, affecting the urban renewal projects and the social-housing expansions that soon followed in the rest of Europe. Today, as modern architects rediscover the principles of good housing design in the roots of the functionalist movement, vestiges of *Funkis* style continue to define contemporary urban architecture.

Functionalism, as a term, seems to conjure up images of strict practicality and regimes of utilitarianism. The Swiss-born French architect Le Corbusier, speaking in Oslo in 1933, warned against the use of the word, contending that while the home should be reinvented as a machine for modern life, it should also be interpreted in a sensuous, poetic guise. *Funkis* architects broadly interpreted 'functional' as meaning 'efficient', designing urban apartments that maximized the use of space through standard fixtures and well-planned storage. The architectural style went on to influence the production of furniture and household goods, resulting in streamlined pieces that were not only economical to produce but also easy to maintain. These were beautifully crafted in natural materials, providing the sensuous elements that Le Corbusier had been afraid would be lacking.

Josef Frank, renowned for the textile and furniture designs he produced for Svenskt Tenn in Stockholm, was also an architect. Born in Austria, Frank moved to Stockholm with his Finnish-born wife in 1933. Although he claimed to reject functionalism as a style for furniture and interior design, he was one of the pioneers of *Funkis* architecture. Frank developed a design vocabulary that updated traditional forms with modernist sensibilities, his work greatly influencing the Scandinavian architectural culture of the interwar period. He was commissioned to design several houses in the south of the country, such as the *Funkis*-style Villa Claëson at Falsterbo. With their flat roofs, upper-floor terraces and imposing windows, Frank's functionalistic villas were the first of their kind in Sweden.

The 1930s was a dynamic decade for all Nordic architecture, but in Iceland especially, where modernist architecture transformed the architectural landscape of an entire nation. For centuries, timber had been scarce – deforestation had led to the disappearance of the island's forests, the little timber available being imported from the mainland at great expense. After the centre of Reykjavík was destroyed by fire in 1915, poured concrete became the main building technique, providing the sole affordable construction material on the island. Concrete heralded a whole new architectural movement that contributed dramatically to the success of modernism in Europe and the United States.

There were few precedents for using concrete architecturally at that time, and the first generation of concrete houses followed the pre-existing designs of stone and timber construction. From the 1920s, however, the structural and spatial possibilities of concrete evolved considerably, laying the foundations for the functionalism of the 1930s.

Sigurdur Gudmundsson, one of Iceland's foremost architects, abandoned his style of Nordic Classicism to explore the possibilities of concrete in a proto-Brutalist manner. Gudmundsson had studied in Denmark, where Arne Jacobsen had broken with tradition by building houses in unblemished white concrete rather than in brick. In Iceland, however, black volcanic sand was used in the concrete, creating hues of rich charcoal and deep russet. The seashells and minerals present in the sand produced speckled textures and sparkling accents. Obsidian and spar were used to cover the exterior of concrete walls, with mineral coatings becoming a hallmark of 1930s architecture in Reykjavík.

In Norway, the functionalists found inspiration in the Dutch modernist movement. A delegation of Norwegian architects travelled to the Netherlands to study the work of architects such as Berlage, Oud, Duiker and Dudok, and returned to Norway with a vision for a functionalistic style that had a distinct naturalistic signature. As Norwegian architects experimented with materials, technologies and styles, functionalism was integrated with nature by establishing a set of interchanges between the built environment and the natural world.

Leading architects such as Arne Korsmo pioneered a distinctive style of functionalism that gained international recognition. Korsmo's Villa Stenersen, in particular, proved to be a seminal house that preserved traditional Norwegian elements within a modernist vocabulary.

Korsmo's contemporary, Ove Bang, found inspiration in nature rather than in the built environment. Bang's renowned Villa Ditlev-Simonsen, built in Oslo in 1938, was a radically modernist building that paid homage to Le Corbusier's most famous house, Villa Savoye, as it took shape amid references to the natural world.

LEFT *The functionalist architecture of the 1940s and '50s introduced the clean lines and open-plan living areas that became the ideals of the modern urban interior. Known as* Funkis, *the style developed into a uniquely Scandinavian brand of modernism that later redefined urban living spaces all over Europe.*

Modern expressions

Throughout Scandinavia, subsequent generations of architects modified the *Funkis* style as other trends evolved, but the principles remained intact. After the Second World War, the whole of Scandinavia underwent social and economic changes, evolving into strong welfare states with generous subsidies available for housing. The restrained simplicity of early modernism was almost wholly abandoned, as functionalism was overtaken by a resurgence of colours and materials and a pastiche of decorative details. New housing styles were rooted in classicism, with a preference for sensuous, robust buildings coloured in warm earth

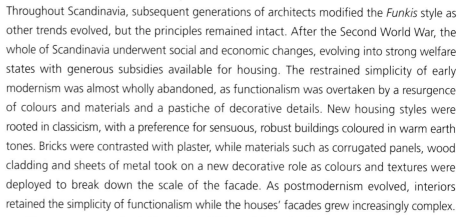

BELOW *Once considered an architectural vision for future living, Villa Spies was breathtakingly modern in its geometric shapes and technological innovations. Designed by Staffan Berglund in 1968, the villa was often likened to a spacecraft hovering on a clifftop above Sweden's Baltic coast.*

tones. Bricks were contrasted with plaster, while materials such as corrugated panels, wood cladding and sheets of metal took on a new decorative role as colours and textures were deployed to break down the scale of the facade. As postmodernism evolved, interiors retained the simplicity of functionalism while the houses' facades grew increasingly complex.

The post-war era also initiated the shifting of the role of the urban dweller. From the 1950s, city planners actively encouraged the development of areas immediately outside the cities, commissioning architects to create new neighbourhoods and often new towns altogether. Suburban areas juxtaposed residential and commercial zones, moving away from the strict zoning advocated by the functionalists. Architects of the 1960s and '70s advocated intimacy, individuality and smallness of scale, allowing clients to shape the orientation of the house and make aesthetic decisions themselves.

The cool, laconic architecture of the *Funkis* era ushered in a vision for the twenty-first century that remains rooted in the functionalist creed. The minimalism that characterizes Scandinavian architecture today makes full use of the wealth of forms and principles introduced by the modernists. Today, Scandinavian life is essentially shaped by urban experience, where new visions for contemporary living unfold. Visionaries such as Alvar Aalto, Arne Korsmo and Arne Jacobsen conceived of a uniform domestic architecture that would easily integrate into the cityscape yet sit comfortably against a rural backdrop. Although outside Denmark Jacobsen is best known for his furniture, his true expertise was architectural. He designed furniture as a detail of his architectural projects, perceiving the building and its interior as a continuum. In the 1940s and '50s, Jacobsen's style of architecture introduced modernism to the Danish countryside, where his furniture also introduced an expression of urban life far beyond the borders of the city.

During the 1960s, modular architecture became a popular topic for Scandinavian architects, who were searching for flexible designs that could be easily adapted for a range of landscapes. Perhaps the icon of its era, with its modular construction and transportable structure, Villa Spies was built at Torö on Sweden's east coast in 1968 by the Danish travel magnate Simon Spies as a prototype of mass-produced housing that could be prefabricated in sections and assembled in holiday camps

throughout the world. It was designed as a circle, within which individual rooms spiralled off a rounded axis. The domed roof was cast in sections of reinforced fibreglass and manufactured as a series of components. Resting like a landed spacecraft on a cliff overlooking the Baltic, Villa Spies expressed the space-age vision that swept the 1960s.

Modular housing is making a comeback today as a long-term solution to urban housing shortages. As the demand for single-dwelling apartments and accommodation for urban couples continues to rise, architects are finding new ways of expressing the functionalist principles of modularity, mobility and multi-functionality. The Swedish multinational furniture retailer IKEA has created an architectural extension of the firm's flat-packed ethos in its *Bo Klok* ('smarter living') concept of prefabricated modular housing components made for on-site assembly. Among the initial prototypes is a two-storey apartment block containing six L-shaped apartments. The scheme includes a small consignment of flat-packed IKEA furniture.

The mini-apartment system of prefabricated modules known as *Microbo* revisits the original *Funkis* models of 'efficiency' dwellings to create a new type of urban apartment. The units are laid laterally on top of existing buildings, or strung vertically into high-rise blocks. Each unit features a galley kitchen, a compact bathroom and an open-plan area leading to a small balcony. Sliding screen 'walls' divide the space into areas for sleeping or socializing, eliminating the need for fixed boundaries between rooms.

ABOVE LEFT *Villa Spies was one of the first buildings in Europe to bring advanced technology to the interior. Remote control devices, track lighting, hydraulic lifts and light projections had previously seemed more like the stuff of science fiction than the fittings of a modern home.*

ABOVE *Bolted to the wall and cantilevered over the floor, the staircase running down to Villa Spies's lower ground floor was a dramatic feat of engineering and space-planning.*

The *Microbo* is intended to blur the boundaries between work and private life by creating a home interior with the streamlined efficiency typical of an office. Balancing storage and living space takes on a new importance as the parameters of domestic space are recalibrated in such a design. The *Microbo* is designed specifically for construction in urban centres, where it can be built in close proximity to business areas. Whether used as a permanent home or urban *pied-à-terre*, it guarantees an efficient dwelling for modern life.

The Icelandic designer Hrafnkell Birgisson is pioneering an urban *pied-à-terre* that is completely mobile, space-saving and ultra-efficient. Birgisson's modular capsule can be set up around urban parks or car parks or can even be docked kerbside, to compensate quickly for shortages of urban housing. The capsule consists of several units connected to existing water and power mains. Each unit is accessed by means of a SIM card that activates a system of hydraulics, cuing the staircase to unfold downwards and the furniture inside to inflate automatically. Once the occupant leaves, the unit folds and compresses back again, receding into the urban landscape until the occupant returns.

Another uniquely transportable environment is provided by Magne Magler Wiggen in Norway. Its Fhiltex-X Mobile House is built within steel containers that cantilever over their ground supports as they open and expand. As the 'house' is unpacked, solar panels, water tanks, a staircase and a balcony are attached to its outside walls, and then are easily disassembled when the structure is transported.

Swedish architects have devised a system of transforming urban rooftops into lofts for modern living. Known as 'First Penthouse', the scheme can magic virtually any apartment or mansard-style roof into a customized living space. The apartments are designed as a series of interconnecting modules, produced, fitted and decorated in a Swedish factory. Bathroom and kitchen fittings are pre-installed, tiles are pre-laid and even the base coats are pre-painted onto the walls. The modules are packed for shipping, then transported to the site, where they are hoisted into place, waterproofed and plumbed in. To make the new apartments blend in with the existing roofscape, the original roof tiles are removed beforehand and fitted onto the new modules at the factory.

In Copenhagen, the waterfront will soon be afloat with contemporary housing, as a concept for 'floating homes' is being introduced there to provide dwellings for urban families and young home-owners. Tegnestuen Vandkunsten, a Copenhagen-based firm of architects, has designed a fleet of buoyant abodes with both working and living spaces. Each structure contains three decks within a painted steel or aluminium facade, topped by a sun terrace and a crown of solar panels. A galley kitchen is situated below deck, with porthole windows placed at water level. A double-height living area is located on the floor above, overlooked by a mezzanine workspace flanked by the bedrooms and bathroom.

As the Scandinavian interior presents a vision for twenty-first-century living, a dynamic domestic landscape is evolving through the collaboration of designers and architects. Working together to move beyond the limitations of 'bricks and mortar' structures, they pioneer spaces that interweave historical elements and modernist principles with a bold direction for the future. With such exciting possibilities for contemporary living on the horizon, Scandinavian architecture is giving 'back to the future' a whole new meaning.

RIGHT *Through clever manipulation of geometry, volume and light, the Persian-born Swedish interior architect Shideh Shaygan has transformed a dark nineteenth-century corridor into a sleek modern hallway. The lighting track travels across the ceiling from one wall to the other side, while the rectilinear cladding conceals shelving and storage behind a rhythmic facade.*

THE SCANDINAVIAN INTERIOR

THE SCANDINAVIAN INTERIOR Period interiors evoke the charms of bygone eras, recollecting the spirit of the timber and stone of Nordic homes. Today, the Scandinavian interior outlines a new vision for twenty-first-century living, one that fuses traditional craftsmanship with high-tech innovations.

ABOVE *Traditional Nordic fireplaces have typically featured a hearth raised to waist level, which maximized the transmission of heat and made cooking easier.*
RIGHT *The parlour at Skogaholm Manor in Stockholm preserves the late eighteenth-century Gustavian style. The deal floors are painted in interweaving bands of Falun red, and the walls are decorated with classical motifs.*

The most intimate architecture of all, that of the home interior, is shaped by culture and tradition as much as by the tastes of those who dwell within it. Scandinavian interiors boast a rich legacy of craft traditions and exquisite workmanship, drawn together in an expression of stylistic harmony. While the decorating ideals in Scandinavia were often inspired by European decor, a resolve to interpret them through the simpler vocabulary of the far north resulted in a unique palette of understated sophistication. In a culture infused with a reverence for style and design, artistic sensibilities also extend beyond the interior to construct an aesthetic framework around daily life. Such visual and tactile awareness is an expression of the Nordic spirit itself.

The concept of 'home' is in many respects the key to the Scandinavian interior. Social exchanges are not transacted in the piazza as they are in Mediterranean lands, but take place by the fireside. While the interior has evolved to accommodate the everyday activities of the household, it also provides a welcoming refuge for the extended family and guests. As an environment designed to be shared, the home brings people together and instils a sense of camaraderie, yet contains the possibility of privacy and seclusion.

For centuries, self-sufficiency characterized the life of rural Scandinavians, poor or affluent. Many families lived in places that were isolated and remote, and hard to access in winter. Often, such households were large, consisting of several generations of the family and the labourers they employed. The entire household usually resided in one room, along with their domestic pets. Living at such close quarters seems paradoxical in countries with vast tracts of land, but the need to conserve warmth in the bitter winter and also the expense of building large houses dictated a tradition of small, efficient dwellings. For simple farming people, these living arrangements and modest decorative styles changed little until the nineteenth century, when the old *stuga* was updated with formal architectural characteristics, and an awareness of interior decoration increased.

In such close quarters, the furniture continued to be built directly into the interior architecture, allowing economy of both space and materials as it had in Viking times. The woodworking was undertaken by the men of the house, with a broad range of vernacular styles evolving throughout the region as a result.

Furnishings and decorations were chosen for their comfort and warmth, but also for their contribution to maintaining neatness and order. In hard times, materials were often

RIGHT *While beds are generally free-standing today, for many centuries they were part of the architecture. Cupboard beds like this one retained heat and left more living space in the rest of the room. The crossed branches and garland of fruit are typical of the Baroque motifs that formed the basis of painted vernacular designs.*

scarce and therefore treasured, engendering the reverence for craftsmanship and hand work that found expression in the domestic interior. The poverty prevalent in the eighteenth century meant that, for a time, the region had to become self-reliant. When the furniture could not be imported, it was modelled on European styles, and Nordic pine was installed instead of oak parquet flooring. As alternatives to the carved panelling, elaborate architraves, exquisite marquetry and precious silk hangings found elsewhere in Europe, there were decorated linen panels, or paint finishes applied directly to the walls.

As they had been in the ancient *stuga*, beds were designed as curtained cupboards, usually constructed in the corners of the rooms or flanking both sides of the hearth. Hard mattresses of hay lined the bed frame, covered with woven textiles, bearskin or wolf fur. Country folk planted enough flax and hemp to sustain their own textile production; harvested in the autumn, these were woven during the winter to provide covers for the mattresses, padding and cushions made for bedding. The beds were enclosed on three sides by simple panels of wood, either supporting a wooden canopy overhead or continuing to the ceiling. Beds of this type were elevated some distance above the floor, so as to be out of the way of cold draughts and also to provide spaces underneath where furs and textiles could be stored in summer. The contoured side panels curved sharply downwards to meet the steps built alongside, making it easier to climb into the bedstead.

The cupboard beds of the nineteenth century concealed the bed behind a wardrobe or chest of drawers. Following the long-standing tradition of creating storage space within the bed's construction, the headboard or footboard often formed a closet, with the bed and canopy pelmet attached to its back out of sight. The cupboard and frame were typically painted in muted colours and adorned with elaborate folk motifs on the cupboard doors and pelmet trim behind them.

From the seventeenth century, household furniture began to relate more explicitly to the architecture, and architects included recesses in their plans so that consoles could be built into them. Narrow plate shelves typically lined the walls above them to provide practical storage and unassuming display space for fine china and decorated porcelain. Deep alcoves were planned in bedrooms for free-standing bed frames.

Storage cupboards were often joined to the side of the bed frame or built into the corners of the room. The cupboards had either doors or sets of open shelves, while single shelves were built into niches, fitted alongside the hearth or simply fixed to the walls where needed. The natural tones of the woodwork corresponded to the unpainted timber of the walls, broken up by detailed engravings or relief carving. The bevelled recesses and planed joints of the carpentry were often outlined in strong bands of colour, while fine lines traced figurative motifs or geometric shapes. Panelled insets in the woodwork of the bedsteads and cupboards were frequently washed in subtle pigments, with the beading between the carpentry joins painted in contrasting colours.

BELOW *Built-in furniture was typically crafted by the men of the house and built to last for many generations. Beds were often set in shallow alcoves and framed by mouldings or lengths of fabric. Many such vernacular pieces remain in use today, lending a distinctive character to the Nordic cottage.*

Decorative traditions

While the interior of the *stuga* was dominated by wood tones, a bold use of colour created vibrant accents in the otherwise unadorned rooms.

The painted details of seventeenth-century Finnish and Swedish interiors were characterized by the repetition of geometric outlines and swirling brush strokes, while the Norwegian craftsmen drew upon their vernacular traditions to paint and carve decorative motifs in the wooden mouldings and trim.

The quality of light in the northernmost latitudes gives colours a brilliance that is rarely found in other regions, animating paint finishes, textile designs and decorative detailing. And because Nordic styles are generally true to human proportions, they are seldom amplified in scale or embellished with bold reliefwork to create a strong visual effect. Their everyday charm generates a cosiness that swathes the interior with a warm, sensuous elegance unrivalled in other decorative traditions.

Furniture and decorations would be established by one generation and maintained by those that followed. As houses expanded from the mid-eighteenth century, social visits became more frequent, and interior decoration played a more prominent role. Furnishings were transformed from built-in fixtures to free-standing pieces, and notions of style and decoration became more widely disseminated among modest households. Itinerant carpenters travelled the countryside in spring and summer to craft furniture for country households, often executing copies of styles or models they had seen on visits to the capitals.

Sharing a long-established reverence for style and design, the Scandinavian cultures have exchanged stylistic devices among themselves and enhanced them with European influences. Their visual and tactile traditions resulted in a legacy of styles that evolved over the centuries, despite limited raw materials and geographic isolation. Many of the principles of interior decoration were extended beyond it to give daily life an aesthetic quality, and although ancient craft skills have largely given way to modern design techniques, the interest in creating an ideal interior has persisted.

Myth and motif

The whole of Nordic mythology revolves around the forces of the natural world and their power over the everyday life of humans. Viking myths tell of humans with the strength to challenge nature and of immortals that embodied the elements of sun, wind, water and the changing seasons. The myths of the Viking era were related by word of mouth through many generations, but were also expressed in rich motifs. The surfaces of furniture and decorative objects were covered with stylized patterns that recalled the powerful gods the Vikings revered, and a range of ciphers that invoked the powers of protection.

The principal Viking motifs were animal forms, especially the horses, ravens, cats and hawks of Viking mythology. The serpentine bodies of mythological dragons, sea creatures and giant serpents were carved with long sinuous curves and intertwining geometric designs, while birds and animals such as seals, wild boar, stag and moose became equally surreal configurations. Viking craftsmen also fabricated a wide range of otherworldly forms that may have had ritual significance. Sinuous beasts with tiny heads, frond-like feet and winding tendrils recalled sea creatures or even insects, while four-legged animals with

RIGHT *The exotic lure of the Far East fascinated several generations of Nordic craftsmen. In the 'Chinese' writing room at the eighteenth-century Skogaholm Manor House, the wall paintings, pictured here, depict the mythical inhabitants of Cathay, idling away their time as they drink tea, barter goods and lie in dreamy reverie among exotic foliage. During the eighteenth-century, the vogue for chinoiserie swept through the grand houses of Denmark and Sweden, where it created a lasting influence, with whole interiors being decorated in the style. Perhaps the most famous of these was the Chinese pavilion at the palace of Drottningholm. The pavilion was built by Sweden's King Adolf Fredrik for his German-born wife, Queen Lovisa Ulrika (the parents of the future king Gustav III). The two-storey pavilion consists of an oval reception room, opening onto drawing rooms on either side, which in turn open onto galleries. Probably the most complete and perfect example of chinoiserie interiors today, the rooms are brilliant in colour and extravagantly mirrored, decorated with Chinese ceramics and other Far Eastern objets d'art.*

gripping jaws resembled the cave-dwelling mammals of the forests. In their trade with the Middle East, the Vikings encountered images of camels, crocodiles and tigers. Considering these to be magic creatures, they depicted them in their own motifs as supernatural beings.

Many of the finest examples of motifs from the early Viking craftsmen were interred with the dead, and have since been discovered when graves were unearthed over the centuries. Brave warriors and Viking chieftains where often buried inside wooden ships, complete with wooden chests, beds, chairs and tables. Motifs also feature in a range of other decorative carvings crafted in semi-precious materials – amber, jet, bone, horn and walrus tusks feature delicate etchings and mythical symbols.

The carvings were often robust, but at the same time were crafted with surprising delicacy to emphasize the integrity of the wood grain or the patina of a harder material. Precious metals such as gold and silver embellished chests and pieces of furniture as inlays, filigree or mounts. The carvings and ornamentation of the Viking era are commonly divided into stylistic groups named for the parts of Scandinavia they were discovered in: Jellinge and Mammen in Denmark, and Ringerike, Oseberg, Borre and Urnes in Norway.

The *kane* drinking vessels, which take their name from an ancient word for 'boat', were presented at wedding feasts as gifts to the married couple. The wooden vessels were carved with horses' necks bent in graceful arcs to form handles, symbolizing protection and fertility. The insides would be marked with vertical rows of circles to stipulate the amount drunk with each round of toasts, and each guest was obliged to drink to the next mark.

Elaborate beds were fixtures in every Viking chieftain's home. Beds were made with a mortis-and-tenon construction that could easily be taken apart to follow their owners on journeys and conquests, and, ultimately, into the grave. Animal heads or magical dragon heads were carved into the posts to ward off evil spirits, while the motifs that snaked along the legs and side panel depicted symbols of fertility, prosperity and flourishing crops.

Many of the Viking symbols were impressed into wood with hot irons, creating a series of circles and lines that formed distinctive patterns. Chip-carving, a common technique in the early Viking era, made patterns of V-shaped cuts, star shapes or spiralling motifs.

The Viking pantheon

The Vikings' pantheon of gods was vast – powerful entities presided over battle and the growth of crops, while lesser gods controlled beauty, luck, prosperity and matrimony. Oden, the god of war, was the ruler of the Viking deities. Oden rode an eight-legged horse called Sleipner, with powerful ravens, called Hugin and Munin, perched on each shoulder. Oden, together with the other gods, lived in the heavenly realm of Asgard, which was a sacred city that lay across a rainbow bridge. Asgard's glittering rooftops and golden towers rose above the clouds. At its gate was Heimdall, a fierce warrior seated astride the golden-maned horse Gulltopper. Heimdall's enchanted horn, Gjaller, sounded a call to warn of approaching danger, rallying together the warrior gods to vanquish impending evil.

Oden's son, Balder, was the sun that shone upon the Norsemen's crops throughout the summer and retreated into the heavens during winter. Balder was gentle and kind, the most beneficent and nurturing of the Norse gods, and a master of runes and magic signs.

Freja, the goddess of fertility, was in many ways Balder's female equivalent. Freja steered a chariot drawn by two white cats as she presided over springtime, flourishing crops, love, marriage and birth. Her symbols were the hawk and the image of verdant fields.

Freja's twin brother, Frej, was the god of prosperity. His extraordinary sword could engage in battle of its own volition, conquering monsters and giants before returning to its scabbard. Frej was transported over land and sea by his magical ship, Skibladnir, which flat-packed to fit inside his pocket when not in use.

Tor was the unrivalled warrior god, the master of thunder and lightning. As Tor's chariot crossed the sky, the wheels produced resounding echoes that could be heard on earth as thunderclaps. His mightiest weapon was his magical, red-hot hammer, Mjölner, which ricocheted back to him after defeating enemies.

Ull, the god of winter, was also a powerful warrior. His strong bow and mighty shield made him invincible. Warriors preparing for battle prayed to him for protection.

Loke, the god of strife and destruction, wreaked havoc on earth and posed a menacing threat to the other gods, but was no match for Tor or Ull. One half of Loke's body was that of a warrior, while the other half was fire. Loke's children were equally sinister – his son was a monster in the shape of a wolf, while his ghostlike daughter, Hel, ruled the land of the dead.

Although many Norsemen feared Ägir, the powerful ocean god, when they were at sea, they were glad of him when on shore. Ägir posed a threat from the ocean depths, sinking ships and drowning sailors. His long, white beard could be seen swirling in the choppy depths whenever the sea was stormy, but on land the sea foam was associated with the froth on ale, and the Vikings also referred to Ägir as the brewer. Ägir shared his domain with the Midgård serpent, a ferocious monster that circled the globe beneath the waves.

Over the years, many of the Viking motifs were redesigned or took on new stylistic referents. Sleipner, Oden's eight-legged horse, was gradually reduced to a four-legged animal, while Ägir's face lost its Viking character as it became the logo of a Nordic brewery. But many have never been adulterated and have been in continuous use for centuries. The classic four-legged, gripping beast of motifs, Tor's hammer, Frej's sword and Heimdall's horn survive in their traditional form to remain hallmarks of Viking culture today.

FAR LEFT *Over the centuries, Scandinavian design has reflected influences dating back more than two thousand years, encompassing traditional motifs of the Vikings and, before them, the classical motifs of ancient Greece and Rome. The classically inspired decoration on this eighteenth-century Swedish chest takes the form of scrolling acanthus leaves flanking lithe lions guarding the lock. Neoclassical motifs decorated Scandinavian walls, ceilings and furniture from the Renaissance of the sixteenth century until the romantic revivals of the 1800s, and again in the early twentieth century with Nordic Classicism.*
CENTRE LEFT *Gilded motifs outline the face of a Danish clock designed to mimic the architectural details of a tower.*
LEFT *In the Baroque period, classically inspired motifs were etched into leather panels fixed to the walls, lining entire rooms with gilt patterns, as this detail shows.*

Painted decoration

Over the centuries, painted decorations evolved in different regions and different styles. Arising from the desire of country folk to decorate their homes, the *kurbits* style of Swedish folk painting developed in the central province of Dalarna. Like Gustavian craftsmen later, folk artists painted designs on panels of linen, but they rarely fixed them to walls permanently. The *kurbits* decorations were displayed on special occasions, then taken down to avoid being damaged by soot. Over time, panelling lined walls and ceilings, and *kurbits* became an early style of interior ornamentation that was also painted on furniture.

The word *'kurbits'* comes from the Swedish word for 'pumpkin', which was derived from the gourd vines that protected Jonah from the sun as he sat outside the city of Nineveh. The style is imbued with biblical references – the images painted on the linen panels often depicted scenes from the Old Testament or the stories of Jesus and his miracles. Because the artists of Dalarna had little knowledge of Middle Eastern cultures, the characters they painted were dressed in seventeenth- and eighteenth-century folk dress, sitting astride colourful horses rather than camels or donkeys. Each painting was encircled by winding *kurbits* foliage, with floral arrays dominating the imagery as they grew out of rooftops, scrambled over houses and spread through the borders and backgrounds of the paintings.

As itinerant painters from Dalarna travelled to other parts of Sweden, they spread the style throughout the country, to wealthy and humble homes alike. The *kurbits* motifs continue to enjoy a loyal following in Sweden today, especially in Dalarna.

Also from Dalarna, the *Dalahäst* – the painted wooden horse that has become the unofficial symbol of Sweden – has evolved into the icon of all Swedish craft traditions, combining the art of woodcarving and the traditional *kurbits* style of folk painting. Forming its name from *'Dala'*, an abbreviation of Dalarna, and *'häst'*, or 'horse', the *Dalahäst* is shaped more like a stocky workhorse than a sinuous thoroughbred, its tailless body smoothed into rounded, robust proportions. *Dalahästar* are carved from single pieces of wood using only one knife, and individually painted in the sweeping brush strokes of the rich *kurbits* colours. (Originally these were Falun red, dark green and navy, but today the shades have become brighter, with yellow and crimson also used.)

Dalahästar represented a source of income to the poor, who made them during late autumn and winter, when the long evenings and sub-zero weather prevented farming work. Until the early eighteenth century, the horses were left unpainted, with the wood grain providing the only texture and pattern. As the demand for the *Dalahästar* spread beyond Dalarna, they were dipped in the Falun red of the Dalarna palette. It was only several decades later that *kurbits* decorations began to be applied. While the farmers were often adept woodcarvers, they lacked the skill to paint saddles, bridles and harnesses, so they represented these as abstractions, using the traditional *kurbits* patterns of sweeping flowers and swirling colours to create saddle shapes across the horses' backs and flanks.

The motif of the horse had featured in the decorative arts for centuries before the *Dalahäst* became a symbol for Swedish craftwork. In Viking times, the horse was associated with protection and fertility, but by the Middle Ages it was linked with prosperity, with the *Dalahäst* seen as a talisman for attracting riches into the homes of the poor.

LEFT *Painted swags of foliage brought the motifs of antiquity to the walls of the Gustavian interior, where they were illuminated by plate-metal sconces hung high above the room.*

BELOW *Gustavian craftsmen often invented their own bestiary of mythological creatures, which they combined with Baroque influences and drew in a neoclassical style, as the design on this eighteenth-century overdoor panel illustrates.*

Baroque & rococo

The baroque style was slow to catch on in Scandinavia, despite its widespread popularity in Europe. By the time the baroque interior spread to the far north in the mid-seventeenth century, it reflected the styles that had been popular in Europe some fifty years earlier. The baroque flourished in grand Scandinavian houses but had little impact on simple homes because of the high cost of materials imported from abroad. Wallcoverings made from leather, tapestries or linen were decorated with Roman figures or woodland scenes, and stretched from the ceiling down to the wainscoting fitted below the level of the window sills. Floors were usually crafted in oak or pine, with the planks laid diagonally or sawn into parquet patterns. Ground-floor banqueting rooms and vestibules, however, often had floors of granite or sandstone laid in simple grids, or imported marble laid in repeating patterns.

By the beginning of the eighteenth century, the rococo interiors that had originated in France set the style for several decades of interior design in the far north. As fine interiors became popular among the merchant class as well as the aristocracy, rococo acquired a distinctive Nordic flair, with vernacular craftsmanship replacing expensive imported designs.

The 1760s saw a craze for house-building that continued for several decades. New homes featured Swedish interpretations of the door cases, window reveals, chimneypieces and wrought ironwork popular in French rococo. Interior paintwork was lighter in colour than that used in France and the motifs adorning the surfaces were even more light-hearted than the originals. Chinoiserie (Chinese-inspired) motifs from the French court were interpreted with the Nordic feeling for nature, depicting leisure pursuits such as gardening and flower arranging or work-oriented activities like harvesting timber and cultivating crops. The landscaped gardens of France were depicted in wall paintings, presenting a tantalizing vision of what a temperate climate could yield. The wainscoting beneath the wall paintings was often painted to simulate carved stone or occasionally to resemble ornate decorations like swags of fabric or lacquer.

LEFT *One of the few surviving frescoes from the Baroque period in Sweden, the mural on this ceiling resembles Yggdrasil, the Viking 'tree of life'. While the style was probably inspired by the late seventeenth-century murals at Läckö, the brush strokes were* applied directly to the surface of the wood rather than to leather panels or lengths of linen.

ABOVE RIGHT *The chinoiserie trees lining these walls were painted in the eighteenth century.*

RIGHT *These wall murals also depict elements of the exotic East.*

Gustavian grandeur

The subdued grandeur that characterized wealthy Swedish interiors of the 1770s and '80s exchanged the frivolity of the prevailing rococo style for the implacable simplicity of classicism. The style unfolded under the patronage of the Swedish monarch Gustav III, who eschewed the excesses of the rococo period and redecorated his royal residences in austerely elegant designs. The king's tastes were restrained yet unequivocally stylish, informed by scholarly knowledge and expressed with passionate intensity. The resulting *Gustaviansk* style still bears his name today, and the timeless beauty of the Gustavian tradition continues to be revered throughout the world.

Even before he acceded to the throne in 1771, Gustav III had been an important patron of the arts. He maintained a devoted interest in classicism, venerating the architectures of ancient Greece and Rome for their stylistic purity and enduring forms. He encouraged the

architects and craftsmen of his court to consider interior design as an element of architecture, and to integrate classical decorations and motifs into their stylistic expressions. Although the architecture of antiquity had influenced interior design since the mid-seventeenth century, Gustav III distinguished his style from rococo and baroque by maintaining the stylistic integrity of the classical era and seeking historical accuracy.

Although Swedish in orientation, *Gustavianska* looked towards France for inspiration. The Francophile designer and architect Jean Eric Rehn studied at the Académie des Beaux Arts in Paris during the 1740s, subsequently returning to Sweden to work on commissions from the royal court. Highly influential, Rehn's work articulated French expressions of rococo within a rubric of classicism, resulting in interiors that were based on strict symmetry and mathematical precision. Rehn's work featured ornamental motifs from the design vocabulary of the Flemish designer Jean-François de Neufforge, such as the garlands and medallions that became signatures of *Gustaviansk* style. Rehn travelled to Paris to commission master craftsmen to realize his design schemes, sending them to Sweden to carry out the work.

After a journey to Italy in 1783, however, the king's sensibilities changed dramatically. Returning to Sweden with the French architect Louis Jean Desprez, and a range of interior design commissions for the Swedish artist Louis Adrien Masreliez, who had studied and worked in France, Gustav III reformulated his stylistic vision. Both men were to play important roles in the development of *Gustaviansk* style as they combined Italianate architecture with elements of French design. While the king never expressed an affinity with the theatricality of French rococo, together with Desprez and Masreliez he conceived extravagant visions of palaces resembling the Pantheon and magnificent Pompeian interiors.

One of the hallmarks of the *Gustaviansk* era was the proliferation of wall decoration. While the grand palaces, stately manors and bourgeois homes of continental Europe favoured intricately carved wooden panels

LEFT *This interior was decorated in the 1770s in the soft blue and white colours that became the hallmark of Gustavian style. The console dates back to 1760 and the kakelugn reflected in the looking glass was probably installed several decades later. Here, the cotton curtains flank a simple valance and are tied with ribbons on either side of the window. Other homes of the period, instead of using curtains and a valance, often draped a single length of fabric around the window, securing it with fabric rosettes.* **ABOVE LEFT AND ABOVE RIGHT** *Refined craftsmanship and simple detailing characterize the Gustavian tradition, expressed in simple pine furniture and understated decorations. Painted furniture was considered to be more elegant, whether coloured in soft pastels and accented with yellow ochre, or merely brushed with a coating of whitewash. As the colours fade or wear away over the centuries, the furniture acquires a distinctive patina found only in Gustavian pieces.*

or flock wallcoverings, Gustavian homes featured flat walls with simple paint finishes. The walls above the wooden dado (wainscot) were lined with lengths of fine linen that provided a smooth surface for painting. Ceilings were also lined with decorated linens, but sometimes ornamental borders would be applied directly to the bare plaster. While wood panelling became widely popular in the far north, painted motifs from the Gustavian and National Romantic traditions still create a characteristically Scandinavian look today.

Given the expense of lining an entire room with woodcarvings or fine textiles, the decorated linens were considered an affordable means of modernizing traditional interiors. Most linen was cut to specific sizes and hand-painted in artisan workshops, then stretched and battened to the wall and edged with wooden mouldings. Many of the decorated linens were produced in multiples, printed by wooden blocks coated with distemper. These would feature a single colour against a pale background, typically a delicate blue, pale yellow or muted tone of crimson printed onto a white or light grey background. Accents of yellow ochre substituted for the gilded leaf that prevailed elsewhere in Europe.

Elaborate overdoors were painted above high double doors in place of ornamented architraves. Delicate renderings of nightingales, hummingbirds and butterflies attested to the Gustavian esteem for chinoiserie, or the 'Chinese taste', which had spread northwards from France, England and Germany earlier in the century.

ABOVE *The understated beauty of the Gustavian style makes it particularly appealing today. Renowned for its subtle curves and hand-turned simplicity, the furniture of the period lends a sense of timeless elegance to the Scandinavian home today.*

Classical borders and friezes were stencilled, with swags of foliage, ribbons of flowers, and sheaves of greenery. Greek-key motifs, wreaths of acanthus and laurel leaves, and mythological figures featured among a broad range of classical allusions, and ceiling mouldings took on profiles based on Greek patterns such as the egg-and-dart. The interiors of palaces and stately manors often repeated the same patterns in the furnishings, draperies and bedding, and in the decorative motifs bordering the walls and ceilings. While Gustavian textile designs remained simple, the *trompe l'oeil* effect of tactile, corded and tasselled drapery painted onto the walls was extremely popular, remaining in vogue until the 1830s.

The simplicity of Gustavian decoration was enhanced by the subtle colour scheme. Many floral designs were delicately painted in hues of blue and white against a background of subtle grey. The tones of grey that typify Gustavian were applied as an oil-based paint rather than in the rococo manner of layering gesso colours. The pale Gustavian shades brightened considerably in the summer sunlight, yet also warmed the interior in the oblique light of the pale winter landscape. In fact, light was an important element of Gustavian style, drawn into the interior through tall windows, reflected in pier glasses and refracted around the room by the faceted crystals of chandeliers and wall sconces. In the summer, the windows were dressed with lengths of diaphanous cotton pinned into swags.

Strict symmetry was the aesthetic ideal of *Gustavianska*, with painted columns often flanking windows and doors, or faux panels used to mirror real ones. The aesthetic value of symmetry was so great that when a *kakelugn* (ceramic wood-burning stove) was installed in a corner instead of astride the wall's centre point, a replica for the opposite corner would be made in wood and painted in the same motif as the tiles.

The furniture of the Gustavian era was generally arranged against the walls, as was the custom elsewhere in Europe. The pieces initially took their shapes from rococo designs but gradually acquired more streamlined silhouettes. The curvaceous legs of rococo tables, sofas and armchairs became elongated and tapered downwards, or were merely turned.

Of the many chair designs created during the period, the medallion-back Gustavian chair was the most popular. Set atop turned legs, the upholstered seat was crafted with rounded corners and embellished with carved flowers at the top of the front legs and on the crest of the medallion.

Armchairs were generally acquired in pairs to flank a sofa or a low table. The wooden sofas that we regard today as characteristically Gustavian are those designed with straight, squared backs and side panels lined with loose squab cushions. The sofas were derived from English upholstered sofas introduced a century earlier.

Despite the relative austerity of the style, a wide range of embellishments appeared on Gustavian furniture. Shallow rounds and long grooves were etched lengthwise into armrests and legs. Classical ornaments such as garlands of laurel leaves, repeated volutes (spiral scrolls) and astragals (small semicircular mouldings) featured on beds, chair rails and backrests.

BELOW *While most Gustavian pieces were sparsely decorated with subtle carvings or streamlined wooden mouldings, many incorporated elements of French Rococo. The simplicity of this desk contrasts with the sofa beside it, which has been elaborately carved with neoclassical motifs and embellished with finials at each corner.*

FAR LEFT *The crystals of this eighteenth-century wall sconce add a sparkling accent today as they did in interiors over two hundred years ago.*

LEFT *Fine art and history merge in this alabaster bust of the eighteenth-century Protestant Queen Ulrika Eleonora of Sweden. The queen has been adorned with a Catholic 'Maria' crown in a witty historical reversal.*

BELOW LEFT *The symmetry of Gustavian architecture was also applied to the placement of decorative objects, which were presented in pairs or arranged in a balanced way. The table sits beneath a wide mirror that doubles the number of objects that seem to be displayed on its surface. The urn-like table-lamp bases point to the neoclassical influences of the Gustavian era, while the silver salver finds renewed expression as a planter.*

RIGHT *This eighteenth-century room has been carefully furnished with a mixture of Gustavian and French pieces. The wall clock and chest of drawers, along with the vernacular chair beside them, are Swedish, as are the low stools and the table between the stools. The late rococo armchairs opposite them are French, and in this setting they reveal how compatible the two styles were and continue to be in the present day.*

The *kakelugn*

The innovation that made larger dwellings possible in the Gustavian era was the *kakelugn*, a large ceramic, wood-burning stove designed by Carl Johan Cronstedt and Fabian Wrede in 1767. Efficient and economical, it replaced the open fireplace that had dominated the interior previously. Before the *kakelugn* was invented, occupying a whole suite of rooms during the winter had been virtually impossible. Cronstedt designed a complex system of flues and ducts that wound amid heat-retaining bricks, reducing the size of the fireplace and therefore the amount of wood needed. The *kakelugn*'s surface was constructed of faience tiles fired in Swedish kilns, typically decorated with a colourful range of classical motifs on a white background.

Because more rooms could be occupied in winter, the house expanded in terms of both the number of rooms and their proportions. Bedsteads gave way to separate bedrooms, and the bed itself was no longer enshrouded in textiles throughout the winter. Headboards and footboards were crafted in wood and upholstered with printed linen, and hanging fabrics were used to crown the headboard rather than as insulation. The hearth evolved into a kitchen, which for a time was moved out of the house into a separate building altogether.

The advent of the *kakelugn* sparked an unprecedented demand for fine interiors. During the last two decades of the eighteenth century a boom in factory production made the *kakelugn* affordable to a greater range of the population. With households able to warm more rooms during the winter, furniture was commissioned to fill the rooms. The Gustavian interior subsequently went on to sweep the country, remaining in vogue well into the nineteenth century. Devotees of the style would argue that it has never been out of fashion since then. It is certainly one of the key looks of today.

RIGHT *No invention ever transformed the Scandinavian interior more than the* kakelugn. *Efficient and economical, this ceramic wood-burning stove circulated heat more effectively than an open hearth, making it possible to build bigger houses with larger rooms. Here, the* kakelugn *sits on a base of painted tiles, alongside a Swedish tea table and chair from the early 1800s.*

Carl & Karin Larsson

At the end of the nineteenth century, when National Romanticism ruled, the Swedish artists Carl and Karin Larsson rediscovered the merits of *Gustaviansk* decor, reinterpreting it with bold colours, simple shapes and vernacular styles. The Larssons were two of Sweden's most successful artists during their lifetimes, studying art in Stockholm and Paris before renouncing traditional oil painting in favour of interior decoration and design. They abandoned city life for the pastoral idyll of Sundborn, a small town in the Swedish province of Dalarna, to which they moved to raise their children. The interior of Lilla Hyttnäs, their red wooden *stuga*, shaped the Swedish vision of the ideal home for generations.

The Larssons' vision for the interior acknowledged the practicality of *Gustaviansk* simplicity, which they interpreted through the bold colour vocabulary of the traditional folk styles of the Dalarna region. The Larssons' work incorporated a diverse range of influences. As well as finding expression in Swedish craft traditions and Nordic folk art, they took inspiration from Japanese prints they acquired in Paris. They combined Eastern elements with John Ruskin's truth to nature and signature naturalistic style, and the sensibilities of William Morris's Arts and Crafts movement in Britain, which had filtered through to Sweden and to the Larssons via the art journal *The Studio*. International and cross-cultural in scope, the Larssons' style was the antithesis of the revivalist historical decorations that typified the prevailing National Romantic decor – and yet it was celebrated as 'typically Swedish'.

Carl Larsson's book *Ett Hem* ('A Home'), a record of the family's life at Lilla Hyttnäs, was published in 1899 and became a best-seller throughout Scandinavia and abroad. *Ett Hem* featured the interior of Lilla Hyttnäs, captured in the elegant lines and orientalized colour fields of Larsson's watercolour illustrations. The light, airy spaces that he painted kept winter darkness permanently at bay, bringing a summer atmosphere to each room. Their delicate tones were balanced by the bold pigments woven into Karin Larsson's fabrics and tapestries. The 'raw' colours (as the Larssons' primary colours were described at the time), stylized furniture and informal comforts that Carl Larsson depicted had a resounding impact on the Nordic imagination. Larsson's images portrayed more than merely a style of decoration – they represented a uniquely Scandinavian lifestyle.

Lilla Hyttnäs evolved to accommodate the Larssons' growing family, new rooms being added and decorated as more living space was needed. The result was a modest family house that became organic in layout as well as in spirit. Generous windows in the new rooms overlooked the garden and landscape, flooding the interior with light diffused through Karin Larsson's hand-woven and embroidered textiles. Passageways became bedrooms, with Carl Larsson redesigning the bed as a multi-functional piece of furniture. By day, the children played freely among the stylish furnishings and artistic wall decorations; at night they slept behind doors on which their father had painted their faces.

The Larssons' drawing room has often been described as '*the* Swedish room', both in Sweden and abroad. This room expressed a countrified late-Gustavian atmosphere, with simple wall panelling, a polished pine

BELOW *Carl Larsson's watercolour illustrations of his home in the province of Dalarna were widely circulated throughout Scandinavia, establishing a style of decor that was adopted by an entire generation of Swedes and continues to influence the interior today.*

floor and plain white furniture covered in the characteristic blue-and-white loose covers of the *Gustaviansk* period. Exhilarating reds and vivid greens injected life into furnishings and wall decorations, accented by the pale yellows, blues and greens of the Gustavian palette. While the modest proportions of the Larssons' drawing room created a cosy atmosphere, the chairs were placed against the wall in a formal Gustavian arrangement. This created a spacious feel while enabling the room to contain enough furniture to seat the extended household. Karin Larsson brought nature into the room in the form of wildflowers, and she also cultivated climbing plants, whose leaves trailed along the wall or across simple wooden tables.

The Larssons' dining room was finished in 1890. With its red painted furniture, green panelling and red detailing, it was unlike any room ever seen in Scandinavia. As in the drawing room, the furniture was arranged to create an open floor space where the children could play and guests could be entertained. While the colours were bright, cheerful and refreshing, the understated shapes of the rustic furnishings produced an atmosphere of harmony and tranquillity.

Carl and Karin Larsson's work presented an icon of domestic bliss. Nowhere in the Larssons' interior landscape does a shadow of melancholy fall to dispel the vision of familial accord. For the majority of Swedes, Carl Larsson's images were aspirational, reflecting subtle ciphers of health, cleanliness, prosperity and well-being. It was from England that such a view of domesticity was promoted as an essential means of facilitating moral and social improvement. While Larsson's painting had been rejected by the National Museum on the grounds of its radicalism, his interior decoration was sanctioned and even promoted by the state. He became an icon of the masses during his lifetime, partly because his watercolours of interiors counteracted the brooding, introspective character of other Scandinavian painters of the time, including Anders Zorn, Gustaf Wentzel and Vilhelm Hammershøi. Larsson's images of a domestic idyll infuriated his contemporaries, however, with the dramatist and painter August Strindberg and the painter Eugene Jansson publicly condemning his vision for interior design.

Today, Carl and Karin Larsson remain artistic icons in Scandinavia with a following throughout Europe and North America. Landmark exhibitions at the Victoria and Albert Museum in London and the Nordic Museum in Stockholm brought the Larssons more international acclaim than any other Scandinavian interior designers. While the legacy of their colour palette survives in the painted furniture, wall decorations and textile motifs of the modern-day Scandinavian interior, so, too, does the Larssons' belief that an interior should be imaginative and satisfying.

ABOVE *In their own home, Carl and Karin Larsson eschewed the formality associated with drawing rooms and dining rooms to create areas where their children could play and guests could relax. Carl Larsson intended this quiet corner of the workshop to be a 'Lazy Nook' where the family could read, play games or simply be idle. But given the Larssons' busy agenda of designing furniture and textiles, family life was far from idle – especially in the workshop.*

LEFT *While most Scandinavian interiors are characterized by simple furniture and crisp, clean lines, some enjoy an eclectic mixture of periods, patterns, colours and styles. Irrespective of its decor, every room is intended to be inviting. This urban interior features an unusual suite of Empire-style furniture made in Finland around 1830. The crisp, refined lines of the furniture are nicely complemented by the rich textures of the hand-woven textiles surrounding it. The corner fireplace behind it is typically Scandinavian. They began to take this refined shape around 1700 during the baroque and have been popular ever since.*

ABOVE RIGHT *This colourful corner is filled with elegant furniture from the late 1770s. Stained in bold primary tones, it is juxtaposed with a wall display of refined illustrations.*

ABOVE FAR RIGHT *A vibrant array of bold patterns is offset by tables of clear glass that allow the carpets beneath them to remain in view. While each of the textile motifs is dramatically different, the choice of colours create a subtle harmony.*

RIGHT *This study is furnished with tables and chairs from a variety of periods, set against a background of bold fabric motifs.*

Nordic Classicism

The irrefutable Swedishness of the Larssons' decor and the *fin-de-siècle* wave of National Romantic architecture created a huge demand for symbols of cultural heritage. National feeling in the 1910s and '20s was strong and it flourished throughout all the arts, finding expression in the textiles, furniture and interior features of the houses decorated during the period. Few of the influences looked Swedish in the traditional sense, since inspiration was found in the classical elements that recalled Sweden's imperial past, and in the country's cultural affiliations with Norway and Finland. The resulting interior was characterized by designs that captured the height of Nordic tradition.

The vernacular interior styles found in houses such as Lars Israël Wahlman's Villa Tallom and Villa Yngström, and in Eliel Saarinen's Hvitträsk retreat, shifted to streamlined, sophisticated decors. Although National Romantic designs had hampered the authentic application of classical motifs for several decades, designers and architects now returned to the classicism of the late eighteenth century with renewed interest. Many also returned to southern Europe much as King Gustav III had done, searching for classical motifs that had not been popularized in the Gustavian era. The Nordic and neoclassical influences merged in a sophisticated, somewhat urban interior, culminating in the style that became known as Nordic Classicism.

In contrast to the Gustavian and Swedish Empire styles, which had deployed classical features to evoke the luxuries of European decor, Nordic Classicism placed more emphasis on simplicity and comfort than on grandeur and opulence. From grand villas to apartment buildings and simple terraced (row) houses, all ornamentation was restrained, with only the sharp, clean lines of cornice mouldings and architraves interrupting the smooth surfaces of the walls. Plaster relief was more common than carved decoration, taking shape in a range of contemporary motifs or in the dentil moulding and egg-and-dart motifs of the neoclassical tradition. The ironwork of the interior balustrades was forged in simple, geometrical outlines, decorated with twisting, spiralling shapes interspersed between the rails.

Considered Sweden's most important architect of the twentieth century, Erik Gunnar Asplund was also the country's most original neoclassicist, and his esteem for the classical inheritance had a high-minded, monumental quality. His interiors had a distinctive horizontal rhythm, with motifs and decorative mouldings elevated to cornice height, so as to remain distinct from any other decorations on the wall. Friezes were painted at the top of the room to trace the ceiling in stylized motifs, and pendant lights took the shape of transparent orbs or glass basins suspended by gilt chains. Marbled paint finishes were applied to plaster columns and wooden door frames to recall the stonework of antiquity.

Villa Snellman, a small villa built by Asplund in 1917 on the outskirts of Stockholm, is regarded as one of the pioneering works of the Nordic Classical period. In it, Asplund not only reinterpreted Swedish neoclassical design traditions but also displayed a great sensitivity to the house's position in the landscape, creating an interior that is classically elegant yet full of quiet wit. Some of the rooms were lined with vertical panelling, while others were distempered first and then either spattered with paint or marbled. Neoclassical mouldings were sculpted onto walls and ceilings, then stained deep grey-brown.

Asplund's contemporary Carl Malmsten rejected the austerities of modernism, remaining true to the folkloric roots of Swedish culture and at the same time the legacy of classical forms. An advocate of simple, craftsman-made furniture, he set up his furniture-making studio in Stockholm and attracted interior design commissions. Malmsten distinguished himself through formal furniture designs that synthesized other European traditions and classical Swedish styles, striking a chord with the past that reverberated in the present. His signature style of decor drew upon the classicism of the Gustavian tradition, which he interpreted in simplified forms. Malmsten maintained a reverence for untreated wood throughout his life, regarding it as an essential means of adding warmth and character to the interior.

The restraint of the Nordic Classical style seemed to anticipate the streamlined chic of the *Funkis* interior. Its elegant proportions, bare surfaces and understated decorations created a hybrid idiom from which the modern Scandinavian interior would start to evolve.

LEFT *Villa Lagercrantz, built in 1910 near Stockholm, was decorated with refined architectural detailing. The villa represented a new type of domestic space that shifted away from heavy revival styles.*
BELOW *Built in Stockholm between 1917 and 1918, Villa Snellman initiated the transition from National Romanticism to modernism in the Nordic Classical style. The architectural features were streamlined and understated, while the decorative elements marked a return to neoclassical influences.*

LEFT *Many Scandinavian homes contain an extensive collection of books, but few boast a grand library like this one. The arrangement of books paints the room in streaks of colour, while the glossy grey parquet floorboards create lighter tones underfoot. The rustic table in front of the bookshelves was constructed according to the traditional mortise-and-tenon technique used by the Vikings, while the armchair and the pendant light overhead add a note of* fin-de-siècle *elegance.*

Funkis style

The type of minimalism advocated by Nordic designers promoted functionalism as a completely new model of living, one that bridged the gulf between everyday living and ideals of comfort, efficiency, style and beauty. Scandinavian designers insisted that form should follow function, balancing luxury and relaxation with the practicality of streamlined styles that were economical to produce and easy to maintain. As the style evolved, a gentle approach to modernism unfolded through natural materials and the subtle treatment of light. In a region where winters are long and, for the most part, dark, every millimetre of sunlight was harnessed and drawn into the interior.

Funkis homes evolved in two phases. The strict minimalism of the earliest *Funkis* homes was quickly superseded by softer lines and subtler details as they were made more subdued in style. In a move to place more emphasis on the treatment of materials, from the mid-1930s onwards architects simplified the *Funkis* approach into the stylistic signature that was followed closely for several decades afterwards. Whether taking shape within urban apartments, grand villas or modest houses, *Funkis* interiors were characterized by horizontal window bands, unornamented plasterwork and plain white walls that curved into flat ceilings. Architectural elements like panels, ledges, plinths and partitions were valued for their dual application as built-in furniture, shelving or screens. Single sheets of glass replaced networks of individual windowpanes, while interior walls gave way to recesses and alcoves. Elegant curves overtook right angles, with railings and banisters becoming gently contoured. From the 1930s, balconies became a pervasive feature of apartment buildings, giving urban households scope to enjoy the natural world.

The Swedish architect and designer Sven Markelius reflected his devotion to *Funkis* style throughout the 1930s and '40s in a variety of interiors and furniture designs that received international recognition. The interior Markelius created for the Swedish pavilion at the 1939 New York World's Fair was a landmark presentation of the *Funkis* style, revealing how uniquely different the modernist Nordic interior was from its international counterparts. Markelius proved to be one of the most important pioneers of the *Funkis* interior in Sweden, advocating an individualistic approach that distinguished his decor from those of the 'modernist machine' found elsewhere. He combined his plain, undecorated wooden furniture with pieces coloured in vivid hues of orange and yellow, which he set amid stark white walls and shiny linoleum flooring. He designed writing tables that functioned as display units, promoted

ABOVE Funkis *furniture was adapted to perform several different roles. Modular systems, like the 'String' shelving units shown here, were easily adapted to suit the needs of individual households. Each* Funkis *design has a minimalist signature, creating a uniquely simple style.*

the use of stackable dining chairs that stowed away in cupboards, and introduced comfortable, streamlined loungers that replaced bulky *chaises longues* and overstuffed easy chairs. Markelius combined plain upholstery with vibrant rug designs and featured lighting designed by the architect and designer Josef Frank.

Frank, despite receiving acclaim for his functionalistic architecture, rejected functionalism as a style for furnishings and interiors, defying the *Funkis* movement by declaring that 'our furniture and our things have nothing to do with the shape of the house'. To conceive of the home in a modernist sense as an efficient device – '*une machine-à-habiter*', or 'a machine for living in', as the architect Le Corbusier described it – was the antithesis of Josef Frank's approach.

The Swedish designer Axel Larsson also designed a living room interior for the Swedish pavilion at the New York World's Fair, featuring furniture with simple, streamlined silhouettes that gave expression to functionalistic elegance. Larsson rejected the soft silhouettes and regular motifs of Nordic Classicism, and instead created a modern environment through the use of bold geometric motifs and pared-down furnishings. Larsson gave his living-room interiors a warm, inviting feel by including potted plants, bowls of fruit and vases of flowers, and he combined textiles in clashing colours to avoid the generic monochromatic decor advocated by many other modernists.

Alvar Aalto and Arne Jacobsen championed functionalistic sentiments in Finland and Denmark respectively, interpreting the rationale of functional housing as a device that would leave the worker and the housewife with more time for leisure and learning – activities that had previously been the preserve of the elite. Aalto introduced the Finnish public to functionalism via an 'ideal home' exhibition in Helsinki, where he presented a minimalistic four-room apartment. With his wife, Aino, Aalto designed furniture for the apartment to function as architectural accessories, collapsing the boundaries between interior decoration and the architecture itself.

Arne Jacobsen, at the age of twenty-three, was told in no uncertain terms by his father that he could not train as an artist. Reportedly, Jacobsen immediately retreated to his bedroom and painted the floral wallpaper stark white, making an aesthetic statement that eventually became the creed of Scandinavian modernism. Jacobsen's heroic minimalism combined a sense of industrial durability with a feeling for streamlined luxury. Like Aalto and the Swedish designer Karl Mathsson, Jacobsen stripped the interior free of traditional ornamentation, but Jacobsen went even further. In his own home, completed in 1950, he eliminated interior walls and even cut away ceilings, creating open-plan vistas interrupted only by furniture of his own design. Jacobsen's radical double-height rooms suspended long pendant lamps and sculptural mobiles, which hung above tile flooring that paved the ground floor in a bold ceramic grid. He enclosed parts of the interior with windowless cross walls built in brick. The living-room walls opened onto the sea front, where he installed glass panels framing the panorama over the Baltic.

In Oslo, Arne Korsmo completed Villa Stenersen in 1939. An icon of Norwegian modernism, it was designed to function as both an intimate family home and an elegant gallery setting for the owner's collection of paintings by the Norwegian artist Edvard Munch. Korsmo united the living and dining rooms in a single, open-plan space, while building the south-facing wall of glass bricks to maximize light. The interior is dominated by a sweeping staircase wide enough to include plinths for sculpture on the landings, and to descend in an open vista over the paintings on the ground floor. The staircase was crowned by an atrium-like skylight, channelling a shaft of light from the rooftop to the foundations. The balustrade was constructed of plate-glass sheets rather than a series of railings, permitting the sunlight to pass uninterrupted through the core of the house.

Also in Oslo, Ove Bang's Villa Ditlev-Simonsen is renowned for its *Funkis* interior. Despite its cubistic shape and the gleaming whiteness of its three-storey exterior, Bang determined to integrate the house into nature. It is landscaped into a hillside, with sections of the ground floor recessed to lessen its contrast with the terrain around it. The interior is dominated by glass-brick walls and floor-to-ceiling windows, revealing the parkland outside from almost every vantage point and enabling the interior to communicate with the natural elements beyond it. The supports on the ground floor take the shape of rounded, free-standing columns, mirroring the rhythm of the trees outside. The dining room opens onto a patio, moving from the wood floor of the house to the stony surface of the terrace in a single step.

Urban interiors

As the 1950s progressed, the Nordic nations began to shrug off their rural past, and the Scandinavian capitals enjoyed a renaissance. The type of decor designed by Aalto, Larsson, Markelius and Jacobsen provided templates for a progressive urban interior that set the style for several decades. As cosmopolitan lifestyles unfolded in Copenhagen, Oslo, Stockholm and Helsinki, the inhabitants began to find that they had more in common with each other than with their fellow countrymen beyond the city limits. Although these cities, along with Bergen, Gothenburg and Malmö, began to acquire an international or metropolitan atmosphere, their living spaces continued to uphold the paradigm of Nordic functionalism.

In Sweden, Norway, Denmark and Finland, the *Funkis* style brought the interior to the cutting edge of modernism and aligned it with a burgeoning international movement. *Funkis* reflected the growing prosperity of the twentieth century and symbolized the Nordic countries' move towards a lifestyle that integrated leisure and luxury with utility and functionality. Like the Gustavian, National Romantic and Nordic Classicism styles, the *Funkis* style united furniture, architecture and interior design in a single aesthetic, and that vision still prevails in the modern day. Although the *Funkis* interior eventually gave way to contemporary trends, its principles of functionality, utility and beauty continue to shape the Scandinavian home today.

BELOW *Interiors of the 1960s were characterized by bold innovations and new modes of living. In Scandinavia, Eastern simplicity was often combined with Danish Modern furniture and colourful Swedish textiles to create a distinctive urban style.*

MODERN
LIVING

MODERN LIVING

Modernity seems a break from tradition, yet contemporary styles reveal the value of time-honoured designs and natural materials. The modern Scandinavian home is never meant to be static – it is created for a fluid dialogue between the architecture, interior design, furniture and the living space itself.

ABOVE AND RIGHT *Discreet storage solutions enable surfaces to remain streamlined and clutter-free because cupboards and shelving are carefully planned to ensure that space is never wasted in the modern home. A natural wood unit can create an attractive display area for household items, or become a distinctive decorative feature in itself. The door of the cabinet above is also a table-top.*

More than two centuries have elapsed since the Francophile luxuries of the Gustavian interior defined a whole era, and more than a hundred years have passed since Carl and Karin Larsson crafted their vision for domestic decor. Yet the minimalistic principles of the Gustavian interior and the Larssons' folkloric inspiration continue to find expression in the modern design vocabulary. Just as the streamlined efficiency of the *Funkis* interior revisited the built-in furniture and rustic practicality of the early *stuga*, so the decorative detailing of National Romantic styles recalled the intricate woodwork of ancient timber houses. As the twenty-first century dawns, an even wider variety of design idioms is seen, expressed in the sophisticated simplicity of the modern Scandinavian home.

Universal in its appeal, the Scandinavian style of living is defined by balance, time-lessness and tranquillity, expressed through an appreciation of space, natural elements and simple harmony. The modern Scandinavian interior is far from static – it is a constant conversation between the architecture, furniture, lighting and the dynamics of the space itself. Scandinavian designers regard interior proportions as mysterious determinants of intimacy. As a tool for modern life, the interior is flexible enough to accommodate the needs of the occupants and to take shape according to the demands of their lifestyle. For city dwellers especially, the Nordic paradigm of a flexible, multi-functional interior is a blueprint for living rather than merely a style of design.

Although modern living breaks from tradition in many respects, various historical elements continue to define and enhance contemporary spaces. The generous windows and the strong emphasis on light introduced in the Gustavian era have been expanded and improved, while the National Romantic style's reverence for local materials continues to be upheld, and the uses of wood and stone find renewed expression.

The style of living enjoyed by the Scandinavian people today can be traced back to the *Funkis* era, when architects and designers created an uncompromising new vision of what domestic life could be. The home was conceived of as a place where leisure interests, social activities and notions of luxury could unfold within a family milieu, or in dwellings for single people and couples. While the living environment was seen as a tool to shape everyday life, it was also intended to be liberating and playful. Bold textile prints, such as those designed by Marimekko and Josef Frank, were deployed to suffuse rooms with colour, and the artworks of the *Funkis* era charged the interior with vibrant abstractions.

Beauty and harmony

The Scandinavian interior today is a gesture of simplicity, yet finds space for brilliant colours, rich textures and lavish motifs. It is distinguished by a regard for beauty and harmony in the home more deep-rooted than in most other Western styles. In fact, the stylistic sensibilities of the Scandinavians pervade every aspect of life, making the far north probably the most heavily aestheticized region of Europe. A deep reverence for nature is balanced by a fundamental, almost spiritual, belief that beauty and natural elements should be the essence of the interior. As the Nordic interior bridges the gulf between the built environment and the natural landscape, design and nature merge with everyday life.

Its rustic affinity with the natural world makes the Scandinavian interior a welcoming haven of home comforts. The warm glow of the open fire creates a cosy atmosphere, and the aroma of burning wood scents the entire house. Having a sauna in the home shakes off the cold of winter, while a dash of aromatic pine and juniper essences over the hot coals serves as an antidote to the stresses of modern life. Underfloor heating warms the wood or stone tiles of the floor, making a barefoot ramble through the home surprisingly inviting in winter. In fact, etiquette dictates that shoes are always left at the front door. Scandinavian floors are never covered with wall-to-wall carpets, but with rugs, which demarcate spaces within the open-plan environment. Hand-loomed carpets, especially those designed by leading textile artists, tend to be left free of furniture and displayed in an artistic guise.

Scandinavian interiors are seldom devoid of sensuousness or warmth. Sinuous, organic textures counteract the rectilinear shapes of conventional buildings. An appreciation for craft traditions and folk art brings rich colours into the home, infusing everyday surroundings with a natural, unassuming beauty. Sentimental treasures are passed from one generation to the next, along with antiques, family portraits and memorabilia, creating a warm union of old and new. Even a contemporary interior retains elements of many periods, cultures, and vernacular styles. While modernism is a mantra for Scandinavian living, there is a reverence for the traditional as well as the cutting edge.

In a Nordic home, the acquisition of objects has more to do with an appreciation of materials and craftsmanship than with status, and the Scandinavian interior typically features a mixture of design classics and quirky craft pieces. The practical, the affordable and, above all, the beautiful are an indissoluble trinity that shapes the interior.

The appearance of places and things – both in the home and outside it – is of great importance. Scandinavian designers contend that looks count less than substance as they strive to capture the spirit of beauty rather than follow interior trends. Designers eschew 'fashionable' ornamentation and strive for the classic, if not the iconic, maintaining that good interior design should outlast its owner. Scandinavian history exhibits this aspiration again and again, as the timelessness of *Gustavianska*, *Funkis* and rustic countryside

LEFT *An open hearth is cosy and inviting, radiating warmth as it casts a flickering glow throughout the room. This fireplace and chimney breast were designed as a single, sweeping curve, countering the rectilinear shapes of the interior architecture.*

ABOVE *Dark wooden floors are not typical of the Scandinavian home, but hardwoods such as teak, mahogany, oak and wenge often feature in contemporary homes. Here, they are used to provide a rich, glossy texture that highlights the smooth surface of the white walls.*

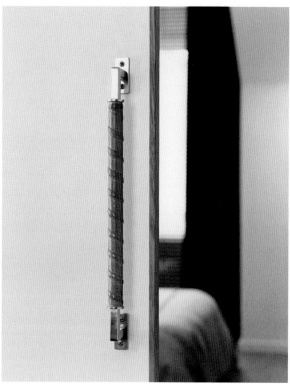

interiors shows today. Each of these styles emphasized purity of form and exquisite craftsmanship, leaving a legacy of colours, motifs and shapes that remain as practical as they are beautiful. While most people would argue that their lifestyle shapes the environment they live in, Scandinavians tend to believe the reverse: that their living space determines the quality of life they lead. The efficiency of a Scandinavian home promotes Zen-like tranquillity, and seems more conducive to an unwavering, methodical mindset than does living in chaos and clutter.

Even before today's trend for minimal living took hold, space planning provided the glue that held the Nordic interior together. In Scandinavia, space is husbanded like a precious resource, with every cupboard and compartment organized and accounted for. Discreet storage solutions are provided throughout the home, creating the means to keep surfaces streamlined and clutter-free. The positions of doorways, corridors and staircases are determined architecturally, with the placement of furniture carefully considered so that the interior never feels cramped or congested.

In effect, the positioning of all objects is a key element of the interior landscape. The alignment of furniture is an unobtrusive way of dividing the interior into separate living areas, while the positioning of carpets and sculptural objects can create 'neutral' zones between them. Decorative objects are thoughtfully positioned to produce a symmetrical effect, or placed at random to augment the harmony of colour and tone already established. Leaving space around objects ensures that their stylistic features remain visible, which is the key to presenting them in a sculptural guise.

ABOVE *While stitched leather makes innovative door pulls for contemporary wardrobes today (far left), soft leather has often been bound to handles and door pulls since the 1920s, as this streamlined door pull (centre) and functionalistic 'd-line' handle (above) illustrate.*

RIGHT *Despite their architectural character, the white flooring and transparent barrier beside the stairwell in this minimal hallway are scarcely noticeable, allowing the polished grain of the wood panelling to dominate. The sky-lights channel sunshine to the core of the apartment, streaming through the stairwell to the floor below and bathing the corridor in natural light.*

Architectural elements

In Scandinavian homes, the ceiling is considered the fifth wall, and in decorating terms it has traditionally been part of the visual impact of the other four walls. Throughout history, the ceiling has represented the skies and heavens. The baroque, rococo and Gustavian periods gave the ceilings of homes a similar attention to that accorded to the ceilings of palaces and churches, but as ceilings became lower over the centuries they became less ornate. In modern interiors, an illusion of height is created through the tray ceiling, which gets its name from its resemblance to an inverted tray. It follows the roofline at the wall intersection, then angles from the wall in one or more steps. Tray ceilings can often hide recessed lighting in bedrooms, replacing decorative features with architectural ones.

Natural, warm and beautiful, wood is also versatile. A wooden staircase tracing the expanse of a smooth wall takes on the abstraction of a large-scale sculptural relief, forming a network of timber almost as intricate as a forest. Traditional panelling crafted in pine, fir, larch, birch, oak or spruce enhances the interior with subtle textures and a natural sheen. Contemporary panelling clads the interior in broad sheaths of wood separated by recessed joins, or lines the ceiling above with a sleek canopy of wood grain.

Where wood trim is used to 'lift' the architectural features of rooms, tracts of polished stone seem to anchor the house to the bedrock beneath it. A rough stone wall can evoke the robust sanctuary of a fortress, while acting as a foil for the smooth, wooden surfaces surrounding it. Upright timber planks or smooth wall panels counter-balance the dense consistency of a stone floor beneath them, also providing a vital source of warmth and insulation that stone masonry can never equal. As the density of stone contrasts with the lightness of pale wood, the interior is filled with distinctive visual textures that could only be harvested from the landscapes of the far north.

LEFT *When Thomas Sandell converted the dark attic of a nineteenth-century apartment building in Stockholm into this spacious, light-filled loft apartment, the brick chimney breasts and the structural joints were deliberately left in view in order to add a robust, rustic quality to an otherwise streamlined interior.*

ABOVE RIGHT *A shaft of wood has been expertly turned and carved to make a sleek handrail for this contemporary staircase.*
RIGHT *The concrete exterior wall of this villa has been curved back into the home to create a smooth hearth and chimney breast with a practical niche for storing firewood.*

LEFT *Varnished timber planks were used to construct this stunning yet simple staircase in a contemporary home. The staircase remains open on three sides, merging the steps and the banister into a single design rather than crafting them in complementary styles.*

THIS PAGE *The beauty of this wide staircase becomes apparent as it twists upwards to reach the floor above. By slotting the stair treads into grooves on either side, Scandinavian carpenters using traditional techniques were able to build such structures without using a single nail.*

Flexible spaces

Every home is an evolving entity, altering to accommodate passing trends and changes in lifestyle. The modern Nordic interior is designed according to principles of comfort, efficiency and flexibility that provide the home with a basis of multi-functionality and the freedom to change. Scandinavians have a head start – architects and designers ensure that they make the most of every last corner even before the construction commences. By the time furnishing and decorating begin, any wasted space has vanished, and hallways, alcoves and kitchen cabinets work hard to maximize their potential.

Throughout their long history, the Nordic peoples have always lived in efficient dwellings. The *Funkis* interior was a modern update of the *stuga*'s rustic practicality that revisited its simplified carpentry techniques and 'built-in' furniture. The *Funkis* home featured built-in cupboards that eclipsed the need for heavy chests and wardrobes, and provided unobtrusive storage that hid clutter from view. Spare beds were fitted into upright cupboards, to be folded out when they were needed, or were tucked underneath 'nesting' beds until nighttime. Shelving moved beyond the confines of the bookcase, and was reinvented as a flexible, modular system featuring sleek display surfaces in addition to storage spaces. Both the layout and the furnishings of the *Funkis* home were designed as a unified whole that could adjust easily to daily changes.

Built-in features are just as popular in the modern interior, where, in urban households especially, space is at a premium. Integrating items of furniture, like tables, desks, shelving and cupboards, into the architecture of the room makes the most efficient use of available space. Shipshape storage solutions are provided in cabin-like compartments and built-in cabinets that are designed to maximize the use of space. A door is typically fitted flush to the framework to integrate with the wall as smoothly as possible. Alcoves supply the perfect home for shelving and storage cupboards.

The legacy of *Funkis* interiors has produced an acute spatial awareness among several generations of Scandinavians, and an appreciation of the interior as a flexible entity rather than a static fixture. Most homes make full use of the room's height, with wardrobes, shelves and cupboards built all the way up to the ceiling. As the city centres of Stockholm, Helsinki and Oslo have expanded, many former industrial spaces have been converted to loft-style apartments. A mezzanine level is often built to provide sleeping spaces, storage or even a home office. A platform introduced high in the eaves makes space for a library or a spare bed, or offers a calm, meditative corner to relax in.

Even in generously proportioned lofts, it is important that furniture and fittings are strategically placed to make efficient use of the space. In large apartments and open-plan interiors, dividing the room into specific areas with furniture is the best way of demarcating its functions. Free-standing furniture, or screens in fabric or wood, are used to separate the interior into different areas. Many contemporary tables, sofas, chairs and even wardrobes are constructed on a base with wheels, making it easy to rearrange the living space as often as necessary. In a small studio apartment, sleeping alcoves are often turned into mini bedrooms by placing large wardrobes between the bed and the rest of the space, or a desk is encircled by bookcases to create a private study.

Many Scandinavian firms have a flexible-hours system or a scheme that allows employees to work from home when necessary. Almost every home has a workspace, or at least a quiet corner for writing letters, paying bills and surfing the Internet. Careful planning can successfully combine an office area with the rest of the living area, even if space is limited. Dining tables provide generous desk space when work from the office is brought home, or when an impromptu meeting is called outside the office. Table-tops fitted under work surfaces cantilever outwards to become temporary desks, and drop-leaf tables that extend to give a bigger work surface are also popular. Boxes of files, stationery and laptop computers are easily stowed in cupboards as the mealtime approaches.

The living spaces of urban Scandinavian homes are not limited to areas contained behind walls and under roofs. Balconies and private courtyards are furnished with chairs and tables that can be stored inside during the winter, while dining suites made from glass and treated metal chairs can remain outside throughout any summer rain. Moving the indoor/outdoor furniture outside in the summer frees up more space inside, bringing a sense of the outdoors into the home.

LEFT *Small spaces must be flexible and efficient if they are to work. A tufted carpet demarcates the living room in this small space, and a curtain can be drawn around the sleeping area for privacy.*
BELOW *A transparent wall and doorway bring natural light into this bathroom, allowing sunshine from windows in the outside wall to penetrate the core of the apartment. The bedroom was designed without a door to ensure that daylight would illuminate the corridor throughout the day.*

ABOVE *Architecture and furniture come together in this spectacular open-plan villa, which relies on tall windows to balance its lateral proportions. The villa itself is minimal in style, with the crisp edges of the furniture and the absence of motifs producing a masculine feel. Exposed beams create a rhythmic cadence across the ceiling, while the whitewashed walls have deliberately been left bare to offset the dense patterns of the stone floor. The banquette extends from the fireplace to the far wall, providing a low room-divider and comfortable seating in* a single structure, with practical storage compartments built underneath. The open-plan layout allows the kitchen and living area to communicate.

RIGHT *A custom-made daybed contours into the corner of this weekend retreat, where family and guests can relax throughout the day and sleep overnight. The daybed was designed with generous proportions that allow both parents and their four children to snuggle comfortably in front of the television when bad weather prevents the family from playing outdoors.*

Storage and display

The living room is both a public and a private place. It has a formal function in the sense that it is the part of the house where guests are entertained, but it is also a private area to relax in. To fulfil both of these functions, Scandinavian living rooms are planned with accessible storage spaces for everyday personal items, and lustrous display surfaces that show decorative objects at their best. Modular shelving systems featuring both open and closed units are often used to combine the two aspects in the proportions that suit the needs of the individual household.

Modular furniture was designed in line with the principles of the Bauhaus, the German design school that pioneered functionalism early in the twentieth century, and was intended to address the lack of standardization in furniture construction. Designed to meet the changing needs of the modern interior, modular furniture has been popular in Scandinavia since the mid-twentieth century. It is truly flexible – sofas that expand effortlessly, and tables that extend in length and width, can either be a temporary solution or be left in place permanently.

The Danish architect Jørn Utzon devised a concept of 'additive architecture' that he extended to a range of modular furniture designs. Utzon's 'Floating Dock' furniture collection, designed in 1967, comprised a variety of differently sized tables, chairs, sofas and sofa beds. The range was based on a system of contoured components supported by triangular-section aluminium frames that locked together at 45-degree angles. Utzon's '8101' chair could be connected to additional pieces to adjust its width or even create a sofa. By applying his architectural vision to the modern interior, Utzon introduced a system of flexible living that redefined the home as a place of possibilities rather than limitations.

Modularity elevated the status of mass-produced furniture, renewing the belief that beauty and functionality could merge in a single style. The modular systems of the 1960s were an overwhelming success. Their strong colours and industrial shapes balanced individuality and irregularity in their mix-and-match components. The genius of designers like Utzon was their ability to create furniture that could contract or expand to free up space or to add more seating. This type of flexibility took firm hold in the Scandinavian interior, establishing a lasting dialogue between furniture and space that remains the essence of modern style.

LEFT *Shelving units abound in Nordic homes, where they are built into the architecture or used as storage spaces and display areas. Rather than stowing items behind closed doors when not in use, or banishing them to the attic, storage can be made visible and attractive, keeping treasured objects within easy reach.*

ABOVE *More than any other mid-twentieth-century designer, the Austrian-born designer Josef Frank, who settled in Stockholm, created a legacy of style in Scandinavia that remains contemporary today. The generous proportions of Frank's 'Liljevalch' couch, designed in 1934, provide comfortable seating by day and a cosy sleeping place for overnight guests. The elegant curves of his 'Klismos' chairs suit almost any style of table, giving them the flexibility to be paired with antiques as well as with contemporary pieces.* **RIGHT** *The Danish designer Finn Juhl's classic chairs and tables combine the beauty of polished wood with timeless design. Teak was Juhl's favourite material and he pioneered new methods of crafting it into tables, chairs, sideboards and sculpture-like sofas. Juhl's use of teak eventually sparked its widespread use in Danish furniture design.*

Eating & dining

The Nordic nations boast a long tradition of dining and entertaining. From family meals and tea parties to formal dinners, banquets and holiday feasts, the home is ritually transformed into a gathering place for family and guests. While the Scandinavians are unrelentingly gregarious, their basis for social life is typically grounded in the home environment. Dining by candlelight with friends makes the long winter's evenings pass in an atmosphere of cosiness and warmth, while the arrival of summer shifts the tables outside to make the most of the summer nights.

The casual style of everyday dining common today was introduced by Carl and Karin Larsson, whose dining room at Lilla Hyttnäs combined rural informality with genteel etiquette. Scandinavian dining continues to be characterized by a friendly familiarity, even though a meal of many courses may be served in grand style. Large feasts often take the form of a buffet, with guests invited to sit in the living room rather than around a table.

The feasting tradition of Scandinavia originated in the Viking era, when warriors and chieftains would assemble in long chambers to celebrate victories or perform rituals. The Vikings would be seated on benches built into the walls, flanking long, narrow trestle tables stretched the length of the hall. Baskets of bread and wooden platters of meat were laid upon the bare tables. No forks were used – the meat was cut and eaten with the knife that each Viking was obliged to carry. At the end of the meal, the entire tables were carried out, and elaborate drinking-horns were filled with mead or wine. As the horns were circulated around the room, songs extolling the glory of battle and the riches of heaven were

BELOW LEFT *Scandinavian cutlery has always been beautiful and sleek. The subtle contours of Tapio Wirkkala's 'Finlandia' serving spoons, shown here, artfully merge steel and wood into a single expression.*
BELOW *Traditional flatware sometimes resembles jewellery more than cutlery, as designers add semi-precious stones to the design. Gunnar Cyrén's playful fish cutlery for the 'Nobel Prize' dinner service takes the shape of green-eyed eels, while this palm-leaf salver makes a beautiful serving dish for bread.*

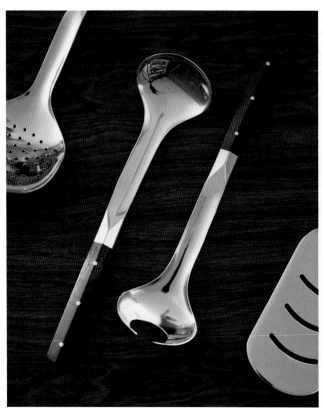

loudly sung. Tales of the mythological Valhalla, where fallen warriors feasted endlessly with the Valkyrie maidens, promised the continuation of these raucous meals in the afterlife.

In Scandinavia, the summer solstice has been celebrated since Viking times, culminating in the traditional *midsommar* dinner that originated as a summer ritual. Floral tributes were made to Freja, the Nordic goddess of fertility, appealing for bright summer skies that would nourish healthy crops. Today, tables, chairs, doorways and window frames are decked in greenery, while twigs of birch are decorated with flowers and used to dress a maypole-like stave built in the shape of a cross. Midsummer marks the start of the summer holidays, when families decamp to their countryside *sommarstugor* and live 'in nature' for most of the season. On midsummer evening, traditional salads, cold meats and fish dishes are served amid a festive atmosphere. At the table, the essential *midsommar* ingredient is not necessarily the food, but the schnapps-like rounds of neat spirit accompanied by drinking songs. Shot glasses are filled with aquavit, vodka or *brännvin*, and drunk in a single gulp. Toasts are made and cries of '*skål*' resound between choruses of song – in true Viking spirit.

As summer draws to an end, open-air dinners marking the start of the crayfish season in August are held throughout the countryside. Guests don plastic bibs and paper

ABOVE *Modular kitchen units have been standard in Scandinavia since the functionalistic movement began. Streamlined modular designs like this one have been popular since the 1960s. They can be fitted into almost any kitchen, replacing heavy wooden cupboards with stainless steel units that are sleek and easy to care for. Open shelves, like those shown here, are more versatile than bulky cupboards and provide display surfaces for china and glassware while keeping them within easy access of other household utensils.*

hats reminiscent of their sixteenth-century forebears who started the tradition. Table manners revert to medieval times as platters of crayfish are raucously shelled and eaten by hand and the shells discarded in tall heaps. Loud singing and drinking of *brännvin* accompany the meal, drowning out the noisy slurping made by the diners as they crack open the crayfish and suck away its delicate meat.

As winter darkness sets in, the Christmas season brings the tradition of spreading warmth and light. For many, *glögg*, the warm aperitif of red wine mulled with cardamom, raisins and almonds, is the highlight of the season. *Glögg* is often accompanied by the thin gingerbread biscuits known as *pepparkakor*, which are prepared according to a recipe that has been followed since the fourteenth century.

On the first Sunday of Advent (the fourth Sunday before Christmas), a set of seven candles is placed on dining tables and window sills. These have replaced the long-standing tradition of lighting a candle on each Sunday of Advent and one on Christmas Eve.

On December 13th, the day that medieval Scandinavians regarded as the darkest of the year, the *Lucia* festival of light is celebrated by processions of white-robed maidens. Among them one is chosen to don a crown of flickering white candles to represent the martyred Sankta Lucia, a fourth-century Catholic saint, whose wounds are commemorated by the red ribbon each Lucia maiden wears around her waist. The girls parade slowly through churches, schools and town halls radiating light and softly singing traditional songs.

At Christmastime, the Scandinavians cook for days on end preparing the traditional *julbord* or the *smörgåsbord* eaten on Christmas Eve. The *smörgåsbord* tradition evolved from an eighteenth-century custom of serving simple refreshments of herrings, crispbreads and cheeses to guests arriving at country balls. The humble *smörgåsbord* gradually evolved into a feast of five buffet courses grand enough for important celebrations and high holidays. Etiquette demands that the *smörgåsbord* is visited at least five times, beginning with a selection of herrings, followed by a second course of *gravlax* and salmon dishes, and then a cold course of meats and salads. The fourth course of warm meatballs and sausages is followed by a staggering array of pastries and cakes for dessert.

The traditional staple of winter cuisine is the *husmanskost* fare. The Vikings' winter menu consisted of dried, smoked or salted meat, pickled fish and little else; today, cured fishes and meats are still wintertime favourites. These are typically served on the rustic wooden platters or earthenware bowls that characterize the *husmanskost* tradition. Winter berries, root vegetables and cheeses feature in the modern *husmanskost*, but the rustic style of serving it remains unchanged.

ABOVE *A dining area can feature favourite pieces from a variety of designers rather than a complete suite of chairs and a table. The curvaceous shapes of these 'Tongue' chairs by Arne Jacobsen echo the sweeping style of Saarinen's 'Tulip' table, which combines the fluid forms of art nouveau with the futuristic lines of the space age.*

LEFT *The wide work surface of this open-plan kitchen doubles as a dining table, paired with tall chairs especially made to suit the height of the work surface. As the cast iron wood-burning stove heats the kitchen in winter, its hotplates reach a scorching temperature that cooks food in a matter of minutes.*

BELOW LEFT *The kitchen storage reflects the open-plan design of the rest of the house. The shelving creates a spacious, open feel which could not be achieved with bulky cupboards. The built-in drawers beneath are more practical than deep cupboards as they divide the space efficiently and enable kitchen appliances to be stored more ergonomically. Their handles have been incorporated into the design, eliminating the need to fix knobs or drawer pulls to the surface of the wood.*

The year-round popularity of drinking coffee has created a strong 'coffee culture' in Scandinavia, with the long coffee-break known as *fika* becoming something of a national pastime. Coffee has been a favourite beverage ever since the nineteenth century, when a variety of special recipes for biscuits, pastries and cakes were invented to accompany it. The informal *fika* was far less rigid than the high tea it had replaced, when evenings spent at home with guests were accompanied by such entertainments as readings of classical literature, the recitation of poetry and the playing of card games. The upholstered, upright sofas of the Gustavian and Swedish Empire periods were drawn right up to the table as tea and cakes were served ceremoniously on fine china and linen cloths.

Today, *fika* is usually held in the comfort of the living room rather than at the kitchen table, but it is still an informal affair. Coffee is generally served in mugs, since cups and saucers are usually reserved for tea, sweet rosehip soup, or the *blåbärsoppa* made from blueberries. A spoon is always placed inside the mug, even if the coffee is to be drunk without milk or sugar. Etiquette dictates that the thumb should hold the spoon firmly in place while the coffee is being drunk, because placing a wet spoon on the table is considered a breach of Scandinavian good manners.

LEFT *Scandinavian style is universal in its appeal. Ironically, the crisp, clean lines designed for the Nordic climate are equally practical for more temperate climes. In this South African home, the smooth, white surfaces are combined with wood grains to add an element of natural texture. The polished wood of the Danish table has a lustre that echoes the glossy white finishes used throughout.*
ABOVE *Displaying art in the home gives the rooms extra vitality and provides a dramatic focal point for any interior.*

ABOVE *The Danish designer Nanna Ditzel's colourful cutlery appealed to both children and adults alike, making it a popular choice for family dining. Ditzel, together with her husband, Jørgen, was one of the first designers to create ranges especially for children.*

RIGHT *Scandinavia has a long tradition of entertaining at home, and the dining room is often a gathering place, where the family can relax together or share meals with guests. Subdued lighting works best in the dining room, and in this household tea lights (votives) flicker throughout the meal.*

THIS PAGE *A white backdrop gives colour impact, allowing even subtle tones to make a strong statement. The photographic work of Swedish artist Maria Friberg transforms a hallway into an art gallery, where Arne Jacobsen's 'Tongue' chair can also be appreciated for its sculptural characteristics.*
RIGHT *Pale furniture and transparent lighting make the colours around them more eye-catching, as these vibrant green and red artworks reveal.*

Colour

The natural textures, pale tints and blond woods of the Scandinavian home create a palette of gentle earth tones, yet colour plays a strong role in the Nordic interior. Whether overstated in sweeping surfaces or used sparingly in subtle accents, rich colours are deployed to dazzle, seduce, unify and divide. Vivid colours charge the interior with a sense of vitality that has lasting impact, while softer tones are conducive to relaxation and warmth. Most Scandinavian homes tend to be airy and uncluttered, with highlights of strong colours used to counteract the feeling of emptiness that minimalism sometimes evokes.

The choice of colours depends on subjective preferences as much as on practical aspects. Apart from its powerful visual effects, colour can have a subtle influence on mood and can even affect behaviour. Bold pigments were once thought to counteract the lack of natural light in wintertime, but the sparkling vitality of white and the refreshing luminosity of light colours lift the spirit all year round. Indeed, paints should not be chosen by shade alone – a painted surface is either light or dark in tone, and either shiny or matt, depending on how much light it absorbs and how much it reflects.

Ambient (background) light is an effective means of enhancing any colour scheme, provided that the balance between diffused and direct lighting is right. When light is delicately diffused over a coloured surface, it can create the iridescent hues of a Rothko canvas. The brilliance of bright colours can appear to emanate from beneath their surface, provided that they are lit from above with a low-voltage or moderated beam. Pale tones are sometimes considered to be the most light-reflective, but bright hues also radiate and reflect light. Poor natural light will turn crisp, light colours into murky greys and will even out bold pigments into a soulless, flat expanse.

Warm colours, such as dark reds, have the opposite effect. They tend to moderate the passage of light and produce a dense, enclosed look that can appear mottled rather than vibrant. Used as accents in a white setting, a spectrum of rich colours can be contrasted and coordinated to achieve a powerful effect. Carl and Karin Larsson used the deep terracotta tones of Falun red, the pale greens of the Dalarna landscape, and yellow ochre to create a rhythm of vitality in their colour schemes, which they set against light-coloured backgrounds.

The concept of a 'neutral' colour does not exist in the Scandinavian colour palette. The earth's colours, taken from the landscape and gently distilled into the interior, recreate the visual harmony found in nature. Interspersed amid soft pastels or colours taken from the sky and the sea, shades of sand, chalk and clay lend an unusual note of vitality.

The colours of the Scandinavian palette are actually more intense than those of the Mediterranean. Golden ochre substitutes for yellow, with red deepening into a distinctive

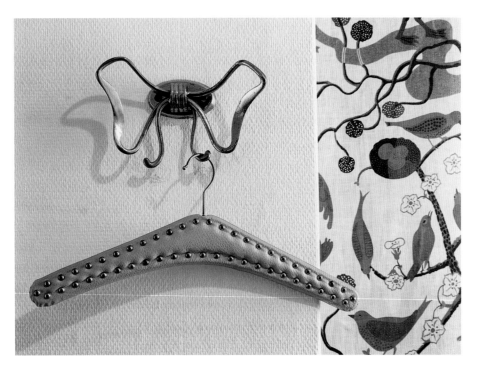

BELOW LEFT *The Austrian-born designer Josef Frank was renowned for the motifs he designed for the Swedish interior design company Svenskt Tenn in the 1930s and '40s, as well as those he had designed for the magazine* Haus & Garten *in Vienna during the 1920s. Printed on fabrics and wallpaper, his vibrant designs made a colourful antidote to the strict functionalistic aesthetic that shaped the Nordic interior during the interwar years. Frank was devoted to natural themes, as this wallpaper section of his 'Green Birds' design illustrates. Frank created the design in 1943 when living in New York. The hook and coat hanger next to it were both produced in Sweden around 1940 and sold at Svenskt Tenn.*
RIGHT *Spring flowers provided a constant source of inspiration for Frank, as this floral wallpaper design reveals.*
FAR RIGHT *Frank's 'Terrazzo' wallpaper reflected the strong colours and bold shapes found in pieces of stone, which he initially sketched out in gouache.*

terracotta tone suffused with cherry. Blue tends to be the 'midnight blue' of the sea in late summer or the heavy ultramarine tints deepening the sky before a thunderstorm. Green fades towards the subdued celadon of Chinese ceramics rather than the colours of grasses and leaves. While brown, pale cocoa and muted coffee colours are strikingly similar to earth pigments, especially umber and sienna, earth tones in fact feature less often in the decor of the far north than in other styles, and never take on the muddy hues of the Spanish baroque and Moorish traditions.

Bright pinks and violets seldom occur in the interior, while pastels tend to be liked as accents rather than as base colours. Scandinavian pastels range between the muted colours of *Gustavianska* and the dusty shades of European neoclassical styles. As in those periods, pastels today are usually combined with white rather than with one another.

ABOVE *Although a Scandinavian home is often sparsely furnished and dominated by pale colours, it is rarely a minimalistic 'white cube'. White walls and ceilings reflect the sunlight, bold textiles bring splashes of colour into the room, while pale fabrics soothe the eye and create a calming atmosphere.*

Blue and white

Blue and white is a characteristically Nordic colour combination, with a long history in Scandinavia. In particular, it was a favourite of the Gustavian era, when subtle grey-blues were favoured, and the subsequent Swedish Empire style, when stronger blues became popular. Blue and white were also united on the Finnish flag when the republic was established early in the twentieth century, symbolizing the lakes and snow that abound in the Finnish landscape. These colours are considered to be more emblematic of nature than any other colour (the association of green with the environment having evolved relatively recently).

In nature, blue is often reflected or absorbed in transparent forms, visible in the aquamarines of water and ice and in the sapphire tones of the Nordic light. Although blue is commonly perceived as a cold colour, it generates a serene and soothing atmosphere. Sky blue holds the promise of bright, sunny horizons, yet its deeper hues also colour the Nordic night, captured in the palettes of painters such as August Strindberg (best known as a playwright but also a painter of some repute), Edvard Munch and Eugene Jansson. In Scandinavia, blue does not evoke the religious connotations ascribed to it in Catholic cultures, but retains its pagan origins as the colour of sorcery. Tales of 'blue' magic unfold in the fabled *Blåkulla*, enchanting Scandinavian children with stories from the legendary blue hills of Sweden.

The 'all white' Scandinavian interior is a prevailing myth. While many Nordic interiors may appear to be exclusively white, they are actually a fusion of a number of different colours. Snow is thought to fall in many variations of white, and, likewise, the colour white is not regarded as being strictly monochromatic. Scandinavians detect many more colours and subtle nuances in snow than do those living in temperate climes, and the Scandinavians' perception of white encompasses a range of fine gradations, including eggshell, ivory, cream and off-white.

In Scandinavia, white is regarded as a warm colour. White gives the interior a crisp, clean feeling without conferring any of the sobering, clinical associations assigned to it elsewhere. White is associated with lightness and brilliance, sunshine, luminosity and candlelight. It is not the non-colour or 'neutral' shade espoused by lifestyle magazines, but a colour that remains true to the tenets of twentieth-century modernism, which treated it as a stylistic extreme. While 1960s Hollywood portrayed white as the sci-fi colour of the future, the Swedish film director Ingmar Bergman used it to symbolize purity and transparency, as his works were filmed in colour.

Combined in a single colour scheme, light shades of blue and crisp whites can create a cool mood in the interior and impart both freshness and tranquillity. They have a powerful presence, yet they do not have the visual intensity of other colours. Together they can generate a feeling of spaciousness, making walls seem to recede.

ABOVE *The classic blue-and-white checks of the Gustavian era have maintained a strong presence in the Nordic countries for more than two centuries, and they continue to be just as popular in Scandinavia today. While the checked upholstery here is almost gingham-sized, large checks were the norm in Gustavian textiles during most of the period.*

ABOVE The pale auburn tones found in softwoods and the flecked grey accents of granite have coloured Nordic homes for many centuries. Their subtle tones continue to be emphasized in materials chosen for contemporary interiors. Although styles and techniques have changed over the years, the appreciation of natural colours has not, and craftsmen continue to consider the colouring of the materials they choose. The juxtaposition of wood and stone in this bathroom accentuates their rich patinas and dense textures.

RIGHT Medium-grey stones outline the chimney breast, while lighter slabs form the fireplace and hearth. The rough, irregular surface of the rocks acts as a foil for the polished stone of the fireplace. Smooth, shimmering finishes have been given to the shelving and trim, while the panelling on the walls has been purely whitewashed.

Natural light

The Danish architect and designer Arne Jacobsen once remarked that 'light gives all things their presence', and natural light is indeed a defining feature of the contemporary Scandinavian home, in both summer and winter. In the high northern latitudes, the sun wavers near the horizon for much of the year, bathing the Scandinavian landscape in light. The changing frames of daylight and the varying intensities of light as the sun travels across the sky cast a range of different moods and colours, making the interior come alive with a kaleidoscope of dancing patterns of light and shadow. As the radiant light of morning fades into golden tints of russet at dusk, evening shadows creep into the rooms, but lamps are seldom lit in the endless twilight of the 'white' summer nights.

As winter sets in, the amount of daylight is steadily reduced. The winter sun does not rise to the zenith, but lights things obliquely. Sunrise and sunset begin and end as a faint glow on the dark horizon, separated by a somewhat unpredictable quantity of light. Whereas overcast skies distil the sunshine into a soft sheen, on a sunny day the sky pours down crisp, clear rays that fill the interior with a few hours of dazzling sunlight as they are reflected off the shimmering white snow.

Like acoustics in a concert hall, clever architectural devices help natural light to strike a chord that is as expressive as music, creating in the interior a visual symphony for the eyes. Skilfully orchestrated, the transparent walls, glass bricks, wide doorways, double-height ceilings, internal windows and open-plan areas of the modernist interior aid the passage of light throughout the home, eliminating dark shadows and murky corners. Roof lanterns, atrium roofs and skylights flood the interior with brilliant light and make the blue skies seem almost within arm's reach – until they disappear under the snowfalls of winter.

White ceilings and pale walls seem to diffuse the light evenly throughout the interior, painting smooth surfaces and rich textures in luminous tones. Cleverly positioned mirrors make the most of the light streaming in, bouncing it around the room, to be reflected off polished floors and woodwork.

To prevent permanent damage to textiles and works of art by ultraviolet rays, the incoming sunlight may be filtered by curtains or blinds at the windows. As well as serving a protective function, these can be adjusted to give an atmospheric effect, or to shroud the house in darkness when the summer sun refuses to set.

ABOVE LEFT *Winter sunlight is subdued in the Nordic countries, beginning as a faint glow on the horizon that casts a soft sheen over the landscape as the sun slowly rises. The windows of contemporary homes are often large in order to capture every millimetre of natural light.*

ABOVE *During summer, the sky is filled with sunlight so dazzling that window blinds and sheer curtains are needed to filter its rays as they stream in. At night, heavy blinds hide the midnight sun.*

Interior lighting

The dark days and long, cold nights of the Nordic winter make artificial light an essential part of the Scandinavian interior, creating an instant focal point for any room. In fact, lighting is as important as any architectural element – the amount of daylight allowed into a room can produce a stark intensity or a subdued, moody feel. Illuminating the interior from above can recreate the brilliance of daylight at any time, while standard lamps, uplighters and discreet floor lighting are strategically positioned with the same care bestowed on the lighting of artworks in a gallery. Hanging lamps in the form of opal shades, transparent orbs and crystal pendants can function like prisms to reflect luminous colours along with the passing light.

Bathed in the warm glow of candlelight, the interior takes on a cosy atmosphere, and winter nights seem far from bleak. Candles will instantly change the mood of any living space. They can be simply arranged to spread warm, restorative light throughout the home, or be carefully positioned to create dramatic effects. Placed randomly around the room, candles cast gentle shadows and emanate a subdued, soothing light. Grouped together, they blaze with the intensity of firelight, while candlelit chandeliers radiate light from above as it is reflected off the prismatic crystal drops. A row of candles lining one or both sides of a corridor creates a pathway of light through either the interior or the garden.

Scandinavian designers work with light the way Jackson Pollock worked with paint – they arc it, spread it, squirt it upwards or pour it over any large surface they like. The bigger the illuminated area, the more satisfied they are with the result. Danish designers often create lighting features more akin to cubist sculptures than to conventional lamps. Poul Henningsen's complicated structures deploy several strata of overlapping blades, enabling strong light to cascade over a large area without blinding the eyes. Louis Poulsen's elegant pendants often resemble futuristic jewellery more than furnishings, while the seductive curves of Verner Panton's lamps recall the undulating shapes of Brancusi's sculptures. Inflatable orbs like Valvomo's ultra-hip 'Glowblow' emanate diffused light to shed a cosy glow.

Noting where the light falls is an important consideration in placing and arranging decorative objects and also furniture. Carefully planned, the balance of natural and artificial light can transform the interior instantaneously. While lighting may be an ephemeral medium, there is no denying that it has long-lasting effects.

Visitors to the Nordic countries are often struck by the prevalence of artworks in Scandinavian homes. The arrangement of prints, paintings, sculptures and ceramics is carefully considered not only to maximize their impact on the decor but also to make best use of the lighting systems around them. While wall sconces and table lamps generate a flattering, diffused light around furniture and textiles, they rarely show an artwork off to best advantage.

For decades, conventional fluorescent picture lights were routinely installed above paintings to direct a soft light close to the surface of the canvas. Traditional interiors in Scandinavia today tend to rely on unobtrusive uplighters or halogen lamps whose beams can be discreetly directed onto the artwork from a table-top nearby. The subtle shimmer of a halogen bulb can make colours appear more intense and even enhance soft gradations of tone and colour. In contemporary homes, spotlights recessed into the ceiling provide an effective and unnoticeable means of highlighting the artworks.

ABOVE RIGHT *The Danish designer Verner Panton is best known for his furniture innovations, but his pendant lamps were just as spectacular as his furniture designs.*

ABOVE FAR RIGHT *Textile technology enables beautiful textures to be incorporated into fabric, which can then be crafted into a spectacular light feature, such the 'ELP' shade by Camilla Diedrich, shown here.*

RIGHT *Erik Höglund combined glass and metal in this design for Boda, redefining the chandelier as a contemporary icon.*

FAR RIGHT *For his 'Block' lamp, Harri Koskinen cast two dense pieces of clear glass, hollowing out the recess between them to contain a light bulb. The thickness of the glass pieces diffuses the bulb's glow while hiding the light source inside them.*

Ceiling-mounted track lighting can be easily positioned and readjusted as paintings are moved around and reframed over time, making it standard in many modern Scandinavian homes.

Concealed lighting is used to turn shelving and display areas into showcases that transform even the most humble keepsakes into objets d'art. Such devices blur the boundaries between fine and applied art, revealing that art and decoration continue to merge into one another today in Scandinavia as they have for centuries.

Light projections have become increasingly popular in the Nordic countries, because they provide the interior with both a light source and a spectacular work of art. A projector is generally wall-mounted or secured to a horizontal surface, with its beam carefully directed onto the wall or the ceiling overhead. Images recorded on film can be projected with the help of an auxiliary video recorder, while photographic stills are easily transferred onto transparencies and loaded directly into the projector itself. The Swedish artist Maria Friberg makes video loops that can be projected onto a flush wall surface, or back-projected onto a hanging panel of frosted glass to create a dreamy image – after all, fostering the right atmosphere is an art form in itself.

LEFT *Today's trend for minimal lighting has created a drive towards simplicity in lamp design, with lampshades and their bases artfully merged into a single form. This lamp by Le Klint is also an uplighter, casting a diffuse glow over the classic 'Tistlar' fabric behind it.*

THIS PAGE *Poul Christiansen's 'Sinus' pendant lamp for Le Klint was designed in 1972. More than three decades have passed since it was created but its popularity has not wavered for a moment.*

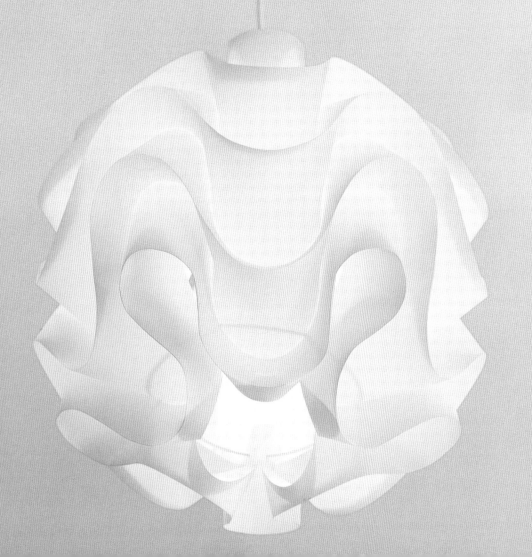

THIS PAGE *The dramatic light source beneath this sweeping staircase was designed as an architectural element rather than an interior accessory.*
RIGHT *A forest glade floats across a vivid green wall as this light projection casts the ghostly outlines of Nordic spruce trees onto its smooth surface. Combined with the Kasthall tufted carpet of grass-like yarn beneath, it creates a wholly synthetic image of nature in an ultra-modern setting.*

Nature

Many aspects of Scandinavian life have a significance different from that in other countries, and time spent in nature is no exception. Scandinavia is a land of second homes in the countryside, and the Nordic peoples are accustomed to an outdoor life. Escaping the confines of the city is seldom seen as a break or a luxury, but an essential routine. The habit of spending time in nature was deeply rooted in the ideals of the National Romantic movements, whose members regarded the relationship to one's native soil as an expression of national identity. Trips to the mountains, forests and seaside gradually turned into recreational activities, with the time spent in nature becoming a cultural ritual.

Today, most urbanites would prefer to surround themselves with home comforts on visits to the countryside, but it is not unusual to find urban dwellers who leave the modern world entirely behind them when they leave the city. As if travelling back in time, they retreat to unmodernized summer *stugor* without electricity or indoor plumbing, choosing to bathe in lakes and answer the call of nature in a compost latrine. Meals are prepared over an open hearth or a timber-stoked, cast-iron stove, where the wild mushrooms, fresh berries and forest herbs gathered from the surrounding landscape are eaten with dinner.

The spartan attractions of such cottages have a romantic appeal, but their primitive character is often achieved by default. The downside of 'getting away from it all' is that remote areas are often far away from electricity grids and can rarely be accessed in winter snow. The exceptions to this are the houses on outlying peninsulas and craggy archipelagos, where it is easier to drive over the ice and to navigate shallow-water reefs by boat in summer. Although peaceful solitude and uninterrupted views are seen as being worth the sacrifice, the harsh winter climate dictates that central heating and thermal insulation may have to take precedence over a romantic relationship with the natural world.

While the pastoral idyll in the forest or by the coast may seem far removed from city life, the country cottage is often the obverse of the urban home. A tiny apartment in the city becomes more bearable because of the extra space in the country cottage, where the family can relax in nature and groups of friends can spend weekends together. An old country *stuga* may become the city dwelling's alter ego, serving as a repository for the clutter, outdated furniture and sentimental keepsakes long banished from the urban apartment. A diverse jumble of 1960s psychedelia and 1970s kitsch may be found alongside rustic decorations or period furnishings, creating an atmosphere markedly different from a streamlined urban efficiency. Brought back to the city from the country-side, grasses, birch branches, smooth pebbles and wildflowers introduce natural textures into the urban home, along with the elements of softness, moisture and coolness that abound beyond its concrete walls.

In summer, the cottage interior is in constant dialogue with the world outside. Nature is not only the cottage's main focus, but its spiritual core.

LEFT *Retreating to the countryside establishes a direct, intimate contact with the surrounding environment, forming a reminder that human beings are an integral part of the natural world. Country skies flood this interior with the colours of the landscape. For years traditional Falun red has been the standard colour of country homes in Sweden and Finland, but the colour is waning in popularity today as white becomes* de rigueur *in the modern* stuga. **ABOVE LEFT** *The terrace becomes an extended part of the living space where blue skies, fresh air and brilliant sunshine can refresh the spirit.* **ABOVE RIGHT** *Big windows bring in the sky and open up the view, enabling this panorama over the waterfront to be appreciated from inside. Designers such as Thomas Sandell are purging the Nordic countryside of the rustic furniture that once typified the country cottage style, making the modern rural interior as light and spacious as the scenery around it.*

Terraces are built along the length of the house to provide outdoor spaces for dining, entertaining and relaxing. These may also take the form of porches, pergolas or pavilions in styles and proportions appropriate to the house and the landscape. Left open to catch the summer sun or draped with awnings during showers, the terrace provides the ideal spot to enjoy the endless twilight of the 'white' northern nights.

Spending time in nature not only re-establishes links to the earth and revitalizes the spirit, but also generates an appreciation for living with natural materials. Modern cottages are designed with the sky, sea and earth as sources of inspiration, integrating humans into nature rather than isolating them from it. As though the structure of the interior were growing from the inside out, the wood panelling is mirrored in the vertical rhythm of the cladding that lines the rustic facades of *stugor* and farmhouses as on ancient log cabins. A ring of fir trees around the house provides an external layer of insulation, drawing natural shelter closer to the environment of man.

The Nordic reverence for nature is also reflected in conservation techniques intended to reduce the amount of timber harvested. Country houses can be constructed today without cutting down a single tree or moving aside the boulders in the landscape. While the position of the trees is clear above ground, the direction of their root growth is less predictable. Houses are therefore suspended above the ground on stilts or ingeniously cantilevered over the earth to prevent future damage by tree roots to the foundations. Rather than attempting to blast rocky outcrops away, architects are building houses directly on top of them and, where possible, leaving their smooth surfaces visible within the house.

LEFT *The Baltic coastline is one of the most varied in Europe, where high clifftops are juxtaposed with tranquil bays and pebble beaches. Summer villas and revival-style houses are today giving way to modern bungalows and pavilions, such as this spacious beach house built on the Danish coast.*

ABOVE LEFT *Kaare Klint's classic deck chair was designed in 1933, and has since become a standard feature of Baltic summer houses.*

ABOVE *The Swedish shoreline is visible from Denmark's Ørsund coast, where the sea is seen as connecting the two countries rather than distancing them from each other.*

Very few city dwellings nowadays possess the immense hearths so characteristic of Nordic country houses, but the hearthside is one of the most important features of the rural home, appreciated for its cosiness as much as for its practical value. After the advent of the *kakelugn*, open fires were used mainly for cooking, heating water and warming the kitchen. The stone hearth was often semicircular in shape and cocooned in layers of stucco to create a smooth surface. A ledge was commonly fitted above the fireplace to hold utensils and practical tools, and an iron rod from which to hang metal pots was suspended underneath. Traditional fireplaces are still like this, but new ones are no longer built in this way.

While electric saunas are widely used in apartment buildings and individual houses, the relaxation and revitalization provided by a secluded wood-burning sauna in a forest are unrivalled. A Nordic institution known throughout the world, the sauna is intended to rejuvenate the body through the intense heat and steamy vapours of its cabin-like confines. It was introduced in Viking times as a weekly bathing ritual, wherein nudity had no erotic role. All members of the household bathed together, cleansed through perspiration as scented water turned to steam upon heated stones. In Iceland, saunas were built within the house, while in Norway, Sweden and Denmark the threat of fire led to their construction in a separate building (though in Denmark the sauna was not popular until the twentieth century). Finnish saunas were set beside rivers and lakes so that bathers could refresh themselves in cool water afterwards, or beside springs with healing properties where the infirm could convalesce after illness. These days, enduring an hour of scorching temperatures followed by a naked plunge into a cold lake is thought to be the quintessential natural experience, in which the world of nature provides an antidote to the stresses of modern living.

ABOVE LEFT *The home comforts of a sophisticated city interior can easily be recreated in the country, taking an urban character into the Nordic landscape.*

ABOVE *Many Scandinavians prefer the rustic charms of the countryside, retreating to primitive* stugor *that revive the more basic lifestyle of past eras.*

RIGHT *The sauna is part of every-day Nordic life, where sweltering temperatures are endured to purify the body and revitalize the spirit. A pine bucket is filled with water and herbal essences, then ladled onto hot coals to transform their dry heat into aromatic steam.*

FURNITURE

FURNITURE Scandinavian furniture became the icon of an era, and many modern classics are enjoying a twenty-first-century revival. The demand for furniture with sculptural attributes that parallel their functional value is escalating, and today vintage Scandinavian furniture even overshadows contemporary designs.

ABOVE *Björn Trädgårdh's furniture emphasized volume more than decorative style, as his cubistic chair and footstool from 1933 reveal.*

RIGHT *Antti Nurmesniemi accentuated essential lines and fluid shapes rather than conventional form, as this chair illustrates. Nurmesniemi's wife, Vuokko Eskolin-Nurmesniemi, designed its 'Piccolo' fabric.*

Scandinavian furniture, with its crisp, cool designs, immediately brings a string of images to mind. The sculptural, sensual contours of rounded chairs and wave-like sofas are envisaged against a backdrop of modern decor, while Nordic family life is seen to unfold amid refined wooden furniture dressed in warm, inviting textures. Timeless, sparsely decorated interiors, with painted furniture, medallion chairs and long sofas, recall the romantic past, while the modern urban home features luminous, lateral surfaces and seemingly weightless blond wood. Interiors like these express the optimism of youth culture yet capture the classical elegance of the Scandinavian tradition. Although their atmosphere may seem subdued, the settings are charged with the exhilarating intensity of a Bergman film.

Making their debut as modernism emerged, new styles of Scandinavian furniture took centre stage with the distinctive shapes that continue to characterize the look today. The designers of these pieces opted for simple elegance and restrained chic in preference to the flashy or luxurious features often associated with designer furniture. The flowing contours of the designs coupled creative inspiration and functionalism with a burgeoning drive to reconcile design and democracy, which found expression in organic curves and natural textures. The early designs were premised on innovation as much as on aesthetics, often employing ergonomic principles to craft the seat and back in a single piece of wood, or merge the arms and legs into one visual gesture.

As the modern period unfolded in Scandinavia, furniture was no longer seen as an isolated craft but as part of the design continuum. Architecture and each element of the built environment were intertwined, with functionalistic furniture considered to be the essence of the modern interior. The combination of building and furnishing was nothing new to the craftsmen of Scandinavia, who had a tradition of built-in furniture going back hundreds of years. As split-level areas were designated in the open-plan interiors of the 1950s and '60s, a demand for a new type of 'legless' furniture that could be fitted into an under-floor level took hold. Sofas and chairs were merged into the flooring rather than into the walls as they had been in previous centuries.

While Scandinavian furniture often bears a trace of an architectural signature, designing it is considered an incomplete art. Scandinavian furniture is often characterized by a balance of form and function, but its impact results from the ability to convey the dynamics of lived experience in static form. Furniture articulates the tension between movement and

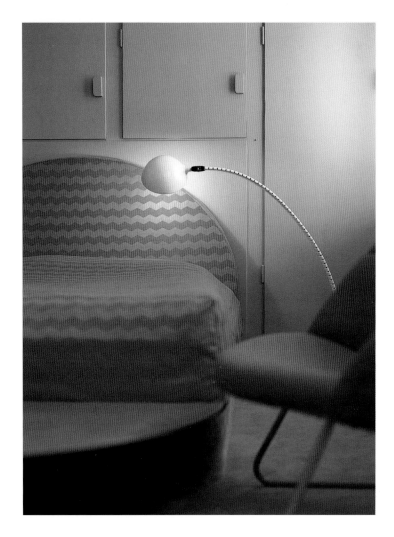

ABOVE *Nanna Ditzel designed poetic forms and delicate motifs that brought a sensuous element to the male-dominated minimalism of Danish furniture design. Ditzel was commissioned to produce this bed as a one-off, using pink-lacquered wood and pink polyester fabric to create a uniquely individual design.*

stillness, and, as such, can never be separated from the human body. Scandinavians regard furniture design as a tactile art because furniture is intended to cradle the human form. Although the use of new materials and techniques has suggested new directions for furniture, it has continued to take shape in relation to the human body.

Many of the pieces express a body-consciousness unknown to other traditions. With seating, an essential consideration for Scandinavian designers is how people will look once seated on the furniture, and the designs are shaped in accordance with the same considerations as for a fashion item. Like a garment, chairs support certain points of the body while allowing ease of movement in others. As each chair is streamlined and perfected to strike a balance between form and functionality, it yields to the seated posture like a glove sliding onto a hand.

The Norwegian ergonomic designer Peter Opsvik sparked a revolution when he renounced the concept of the stationary chair, concluding that sitting is a mode of action rather than a passive exercise. Even when seated, the body is constantly in motion, and the ideal chair should accommodate the body rather than restrict it. Scandinavian chairs and sofas are designed to centre and balance the posture from every direction; as the chair back cradles the spine, the chair arms extend to support the elbows and forearms, or disappear entirely to facilitate a greater range of movement for the seated form.

Chairs were often crafted into abstractions of nature, a design feature that became for a brief time a hallmark of Scandinavian furniture. Arne Jacobsen recreated the perfect curves of the eggshell and captured the grace of the swan in two of his club chairs, as well as profiling a stackable chair on the outline of an ant. Bruno Mathsson contorted armrests and chair legs into a grasshopper's silhouette, while Mattias Ljunggren's 'Cobra' recalls the sweeping movement of a snake rearing to strike. Nanna Ditzel designed delicate wings for her 'Butterfly' chair, which she set atop legs that bend gently at the 'knees'. (For more about some of these designs, see pages 130–133.)

Scandinavian furniture has a long history of symbolic references and allegorical meanings. Expressions of nationalism took shape in the ornate furniture of revival styles and in the heavy materials of the National Romantic movement. To Carl and Karin Larsson, progressive furnishings embodied the search for a better life, and the quest to transform the home encompassed the values of those who dwelt in it.

As furniture began to represent political sensibilities and lifestyle aspirations, it engendered an appreciation of simple beauty and the aesthetic value of natural materials, shaking off furniture's snobbish associations and aligning it with comfort and functionality. This modern approach undermined the legacy of elitist values introduced by Gustavian style, which, incredibly, had dominated the arts and crafts output in Sweden ever since it was established in the second half of the eighteenth century.

The beauty, comfort, luxury and utility that continue to be expressed in Scandinavian furniture today show that furniture is no longer categorized as either an antique relic or a purely practical tool, as it was during the Gustavian era, but is instead conceived as the means of creating a comfort zone for living. Following Carl and Karin Larsson's domestic vision, the Swedish social reformer Ellen Key revealed the extent to which the benefits of design contribute to the mood and satisfaction of living. Good design should not be seen as a luxury, Key insisted, but as a necessity.

Key's seminal text, *Skönhet för Alla*, or '*Beauty for All*', published in 1899, outlined the need for reforms to the standard of living, which she claimed could be achieved through new standards of design. Key's appeal for 'more beautiful things for everyday use' became the manifesto of the *Svenska Slöjdförening* – the Swedish Craft Association – which put her theory to work. The young designers of Key's era, such as Carl Malmsten, Sven Markelius, Axel Larsson and Bruno Mathsson, coupled simplicity with the determination to make high-quality furniture that was not only aesthetically pleasing but also affordable. And in the hands of other Scandinavian designers such as Alvar Aalto, Arne Jacobsen and Finn Juhl, the style was both ultra-modern and easily affordable, remaining within reach of most of the population.

Danish furniture attracted international attention as the Danish Modern movement became a global phenomenon in the 1950s. Subtle influences from English Regency furniture, American Shaker chairs and Bauhaus precepts gave Danish furniture a signature style that differentiated it from its Scandinavian counterparts. Ever since the eighteenth century, when furniture-makers began training at the Royal Danish Academy of Fine Arts in Copenhagen, craft techniques in Denmark have been distinct from those in the other Nordic nations. Whereas Swedish and Norwegian furniture was crafted by master carpenters, Danish furniture was shaped by the cross-fertilization of artists, designers and cabinetmakers training at the academy.

As the exhibition Design in Scandinavia began its tour of North America in 1954, Danish furniture, along with glass, ceramics, metalware and well-designed pieces from the other Nordic nations, was interpreted as a single style. This was the first time that the Scandinavian countries were presented together in a collective aesthetic, and the concept of a generic 'Scandinavian style' took hold, to the bewilderment of the designers and their public back in Europe. As Design in Scandinavia took North America by storm, films and courses accompanied the exhibition, and newspapers and magazines reported on the show continuously. At the time, the culture of suburban living was growing in appeal, and North America's middle classes were seeking an aesthetic orientation.

BELOW *Alvar Aalto devised simple designs in weightless blond wood that created new directions for furniture. Emphasizing comfort and utility, he stripped away prevailing ideas about what furniture should be. Aalto pioneered the technique of bending wood into flowing shapes merging the vertical and horizontal elements. This table and set of chairs, like much of his furniture, have remained in production since they were first made, proving that his work was not an isolated style but a forerunner of contemporary design.*

The Americans, won over by the style's European flair and touch of nature, embraced the ideal of the unpretentious, modern domestic environment that it seemed to represent.

The products on exhibit attracted the interest of department stores, whose initial orders reflected the tastes of the exhibition curators more than the design output of the Nordic nations. They turned to Finland for glassware and flatware, Sweden for textiles and glass, Norway for handicrafts – and Denmark for furniture. The demand for Danish furniture skyrocketed and the Danes were quick to react, establishing furniture workshops and chair factories that transformed a cottage industry into a commercial success virtually overnight.

With the Danish Modern wave sweeping through Europe and parts of the Far East as it did through North America, furniture became the epitome of Danish design. For centuries, Denmark, as a maritime nation, had excelled at exporting goods produced with a high degree of craftsmanship. Denmark's tradition of cabinetmaking was more advanced than that of any other Scandinavian nation, providing an established culture of design for modern furniture-makers to draw upon. As the designers succeeded in taking old traditions to a new height, the Danish Modern movement evolved by expressing organization and efficiency in simple, yet elegant furniture made from wood.

Modern innovation

With a unique tradition of furniture crafted by carvers and woodworkers, the Norwegians have always harboured a strong suspicion of bourgeois furniture, preferring vernacular styles that had been wrought in a vast range of local timbers. Iceland, on the other hand, having few raw materials, was forced to emphasize durability and economy of design instead. Only recently have Icelandic designers begun to produce furniture intended to compete with its counterparts from elsewhere in Scandinavia. In the 1950s and '60s, an embargo on importing furniture into Iceland enabled several small furniture workshops to establish a domestic market. During this time, designers demonstrated an unrivalled ability to take inspiration from existing forms and adapt them into something unique.

Finnish furniture has occasionally been criticized by the other Nordic nations for the elitism associated with its one-off studio pieces, but, in fact, Finland, like its neighbours, also produces a wide range of democratic pieces manufactured in multiples. While Finland's spectrum of mass-produced furniture is on a par with other Scandinavian designs, its 'exclusive' studio pieces help to perpetuate the craft and carpentry techniques that have characterized Finnish furniture for centuries.

Today, Scandinavian furniture designers continue to produce timeless pieces, but also look ahead to try to anticipate how the future will unfold. In the same way that the unadorned decor of the *Funkis* movement gave way to the ultra-modern interior of the jet age, technological advances enable designers to create visionary designs by reconfiguring classical materials or exploring new ones altogether. As a new generation of designers take existing concepts of Scandinavian furniture forward, they demonstrate the same ability to break new ground as their mentors once did. The beauty and aesthetic harmony of their designs, together with their high-quality materials and workmanship, preserve the unique character of Scandinavian furniture in the twenty-first century.

ABOVE RIGHT *Yngve Ekström's 'Lamino' chair and footstool perfectly capture the mood of Scandinavian furniture design today: beautiful, comfortable, streamlined and sleek.*

ABOVE FAR RIGHT *Bruno Mathsson was one of the greatest pioneers of modern Swedish furniture. Designs like the 'Eva' chair shown here echoed the contours of the human body to provide comfort and support. Mathsson developed this ergonomic vision of design as early as the 1930s.*

RIGHT *Poul Volther designed furniture from an architectural perspective, creating numerous chairs in wood and metal. This teak chair from the 1950s is a radical reworking of the traditional ladder-back chair, which he angled backwards to form an easy chair.*

FAR RIGHT *Poul Kjærholm's 'PK22' chair celebrates its fiftieth anniversary in 2005, yet looks completely contemporary today. Destined to be a design classic, the 'PK22' is already an icon of steel furniture.*

Versatile wood

Sensuous and sublime, wood has a presence that surpasses the appeal of other materials. When it is crafted into furniture, its beauty and versatility reveal the mysteries of nature through the techniques of design. As a medium, wood is equated with permanence – it is as durable and long-lasting as it is practical and good-looking. The range of subtle colours and fine grains means that each piece is different; every item of wooden furniture has the cachet of being unique.

Precious to Nordic furniture craftsmen are light-toned woods with honey-coloured hues or crisp grains tinted in shades of subtle pink. Of these, birch, spruce, fir, pine and beech have always been especially treasured. Oak, elm and ash, with their dense mass and deep, fine grains, become lustrous in tone when polished to a high sheen. Hardwoods such as birch and alder were chosen for their durability, translucent colour and satin finish.

Since Viking times, the Nordic peoples have revered wood for its beautiful grains and aromatic properties. For many years, wood was virtually the only raw material that could be accessed easily, and the Viking craftsmen were world leaders for their ingenious methods of tooling it. Viking shipwrights perfected the art of watertight joinery, leaving a legacy of techniques that can transform several separate pieces into a single entity. To the Vikings, the craftsmanship of a well-built boat exemplified the principles of form, function and beauty. The fitted furnishings of the hold and the carved detail of the prow became the inheritance of medieval cabinetmakers, who perfected their techniques for following generations.

The seventeenth-century woodworkers of Scandinavia surpassed the skills of European craftsmen in their tooling techniques. At this time, Denmark boasted a maritime trade industry that exported its cabinets to other parts of Europe, and imported precious woods from the Far East. While the furniture of great European cabinetmakers was often merely varnished and adorned with finials, Danish craftsmen took delight in finishing their works with intricate carvings, panel inlays and delicate trims. The door jambs of cupboards and cabinets were subtly contoured, and fitted with doors that closed flush against the surface. The frames of tables, chairs and beds fitted together by mitred halving joints concealed among subtle moulding carved into the wood.

Veneers were planed from elaborately patterned wood grains or burl, and expertly joined to the surface. The pieces were typically finished with a glossy sheen achieved through repeated applications of a mixture of oils and lacquer, which were buffed entirely by hand. The lacquered surfaces lent themselves to further embellishment, and fine furniture was often finished with swirling patterns, filigree etchings or motifs applied in gold leaf.

When the mid-twentieth-century craze for Scandinavian furniture took hold, the Danes responded with the same alacrity as their maritime forebears. Furniture craftsmen looked to the great northern forests of Sweden, Finland and Norway for birch, larch and elm, and evergreens such as pine, spruce and fir. Denmark's own beech forests provided rosy-hued, pliable wood well suited to steam bending, while Danish craftsmen imported tropical hardwoods such as teak, mahogany and wenge from the Far East. For several decades, Denmark was the chief European importer of teak. Teak had previously been associated more with luxury than with vernacular styles or functionality, but by the 1950s and '60s teak furniture was virtually the hallmark of the Danish Modern style.

LEFT The subtle beauty and lustrous patina of wood make it the material of choice for every furniture craftsman. Its durability and strength give wood a timeless quality rarely found in other natural materials. Josef Frank gave this chest of drawers a veneer of luxurious North American sequoia wood set within a framework of solid walnut. Although the piece was initially named the 'Twenty-one Drawer Cupboard', the final design resulted in only nineteen drawers as the overall proportions were downscaled.

BELOW *Børge Mogensen's design vocabulary ranged from American Shaker influences to ergonomic forms, but each piece of furniture he designed reflected the expertise of the Danish cabinetmakers who worked alongside him. The fine craftsmanship and masculine proportions of the beech table pictured here are typical of his distinctive style.*

RIGHT *In interiors, wood is used to shape architectural features. Panelling and wood surfaces reconfigure the decor as they form a skin over the walls, giving rooms an expressive value that is independent of the architecture behind them.*

Widely used in Denmark for centuries, beech has more recently gained currency in other parts of Scandinavia. Its strength and density make it resistant to abrasive wear, and the reddish tinge of its light sapwood gives beech furniture a subtle, warm, rosy tint. Beech is a wood with a long, illustrious past that can be traced back to the ancient tribes of Central Asia, who stripped its pliable bark away and carved the first written language into its surface. Its bark continues to be used today in a range of vernacular Scandinavian furniture, while the uniform, straight-grained pattern of its heartwood makes it a popular choice for table surfaces, chests, shelving and beds.

Because it has a fine, smooth texture and a polished surface that can be worked to a shimmering finish, pine has been prized since ancient times for making furniture. Its pale yellow grain and aromatic fragrance give it a distinctive appeal. Pine trees generally grow evenly and straight, making them easy to harvest and economical to convert into timber. The bulk of the Scandinavian furniture in today's market is crafted from pine, the material of choice for mass-produced pieces and flat-pack furniture. Historically, pine furniture was left untreated and polished to a subtle sheen, but during the Gustavian era it was painted or whitewashed. Today, pine furniture continues to be painted, or is stained with translucent colours that allow the beauty of its grain to shine through.

Birch is another light-coloured wood and probably the most common hardwood in Scandinavia. Seldom stained, it is usually coated with a clear layer of uncoloured lacquer to emphasize its silky shimmer. There are two different species, the silver birch (*Betula pendula*) and the white birch (*Betula pubescens*). Both woods are light-coloured, with a thin grain that ranges from straight lines to flame-like curves, but the white birch has a straighter grain.

Like birch, larch is characterized by beautiful flame-like patterns, its tight grain contorting into small knots. Freshly harvested larch resembles birch, rivalling it in beauty and lustre, until its heartwood is exposed to sunlight and gradually deepens into a silvery-grey or charcoal colour.

Oak is one of the toughest woods found in the Nordic climate. Hard and dense, it is suitable for heavy furniture or pieces made to withstand wear and tear. It is pliable when subjected to steam-bending processes, but otherwise oak is impervious to liquids, making it a popular choice for kitchen surfaces and dining tables. Its sapwood is light-coloured while its heartwood is light to dark brown.

Ash is one of the most pliable woods used in Scandinavian furniture. With its high resilience and remarkable elasticity, it is ideal for the curvaceous seats and backrests of chairs or other wavy furniture. Ash is straight-grained and dense, but it is susceptible to fungal and beetle attack, both of which leave lasting traces in the grain. White ash has a clear white sapwood that may deepen to pale yellow in places, with a heartwood that deepens to beige or medium-brown tones.

Elm is as durable as ash is pliable. Thin veneers of elm can be steamed into broad curves, but its dense, interlocking grain makes it

difficult to splice. Elm has a greyish-white to light brown sapwood, with heartwood that is reddish brown to dark brown in colour. The hefty wood from its thickest roots can also be used in cabinet construction, its dense surface polished to a rich lustre.

Alder is also an excellent wood for cabinetmaking. With its rich reddish colour and beautiful black markings, it is ideal for use as a veneer, while its density suits it to deep carving. Alder's relative softness and its resistance to shrinkage and swelling make it perfect for drawers and flush cupboard doors.

Irrespective of their different grains, all types of wood speak a common language of simplicity and beauty. Wood is comfortable, homey and inviting, and can warm the spirit as much as it does the atmosphere of a room. Although furniture designs continue to evolve, the allure of natural wood seems never to fade.

Modern classics

When the 'far out' furniture of the rock-and-roll generation started making an appearance in antiques shops, it was not a sign of its old age so much as a statement of style. In the short period between the advent of functionalism after the First World War and the style revolution of the 1960s, Scandinavian designers produced some of the most significant furniture of the twentieth century. The pieces are often described today as timeless designs, modern classics or contemporary legends, and many are regarded as the next generation of antiques.

Despite its understated forms and its lack of hyperbole, vintage Scandinavian furniture has defied the cult of the collectable to increase in value and also in appeal as the years go by. Perhaps it is the plainness and simplicity of the designs that make them look contemporary today. Some have remained in continuous production since the 1920s and '30s. When a resurgence of minimalism gripped the 1990s, classic furniture designs from the 1940s, '50s and '60s were reintroduced to an audience around the globe. The designers themselves also gained recognition outside the Nordic countries, and retrospective shows of key Scandinavian designers have toured the world.

The modern classics made by Nordic designers captured the mid-century spirit in powerful expressions of functionalist designs. These designers shrugged off the legacy of awkward heaviness and rigid angles left behind by the neoclassicism and revival styles of the late nineteenth century. Eschewing the notion that chairs, tables and sofas should be designed strictly as interior accessories, Scandinavian modernists determined to redefine furniture as unique statements of design. Spurred on to produce furniture that could appropriately furnish the modern interior, they crafted simple pieces that had a resounding impact on their streamlined surroundings. The minimalistic designs of the *Funkis* era were conceived as the first pieces of modern furniture, and were intended to remain contemporary throughout their lifespan.

LEFT *Nordic homes rarely feature a matching set of dining furniture. Most make an individual statement with a table selected to suit chairs that have been chosen for their comfort or design innovation, or a table that deliberately contrasts with the chairs. The contemporary drop-leaf table shown here, based on an early Gustavian design, is flanked by original 'Ant' chairs designed by Arne Jacobsen in the 1950s. The 'Ant' chair model shown here evolved from the original '3100' three-legged version. Reportedly Jacobsen was outraged when the manufacturer insisted on adding the fourth leg.*

Scandinavian furniture of the 1940s, '50s and '60s was iconic in its stark minimalism, which pared decorative features down to the simplest possible statement. Designers such as Arne Jacobsen, Alvar Aalto, Bruno Mathsson and Finn Juhl peeled away layers of upholstery, padding and springs to bring the underlying supports directly into view. The furniture's structure was sparse and simple, with new construction techniques making it possible to craft frameworks that were pleasing to the eye. Since they were no longer designed to conceal a complex inner core, surfaces became streamlined and sleek. While their designs embody the spirit of an era, they are typically unblemished by the ornamentation, motifs and patterned fabrics that 'date' furniture for ever.

To foreign admirers, Scandinavian furniture design for many years centred around the chair. Elsewhere in the world, chairs were created for the sole purpose of providing seating, and were stylized according to the prevailing tastes of the day. Nordic designers determined to move beyond the perception of a chair as merely a functional object, by pioneering visions of how it could be assigned new roles. Although classical chairs also doubled as impromptu clothes racks, bedside tables, temporary bookshelves and stepladders, they were not made with the versatility of other decorative objects. The designers therefore looked into methods of creating enduring, multi-functional designs.

Old-school furniture craftsmen believed that chairs required four legs and an imposing back to be sturdy, but this made them too bulky to stow away in cupboards, and awkward to move. As the Danish architect and designer Arne Jacobsen's early visions of tubular-steel chairs gradually gave way to lightweight club chairs, he used bent plywood to craft feather-light chairs that were not only unobtrusive and stackable, but also practical, comfortable and durable. Designs like the '*Myren*', or 'Ant', chair, which virtually became Jacobsen's design signature, were streamlined into weightless silhouettes. The 'Ant' chair was designed with only two parts: a seat and three interconnected legs. It used the minimum amount of materials, making construction easy and economical. More than a million 'Ant' chairs have been sold since, in a range of different colours and finishes. The 'Ant' colour palette was introduced by the manufacturer after Jacobsen's death. Jacobsen, a purist, would never have allowed his design to be adulterated by paint or surface motifs.

The 'Ant' was followed by the 'Tongue' chair and the 'Series 7' chairs, also made from bent plywood and designed with an emphasis on verticality and weightlessness. All of Jacobsen's chairs were characterized by a unique 'floating' effect that refuted the actual weight and density of the furniture. He made pedestal bases for chairs and tables to eliminate the sprawl of legs, redefining their undercarriage as a single gesture. To Jacobsen's eye, a slender pedestal created a sense of rest not possible in a sea of angled lines. He crafted legs and pedestal bases as thin as structurally possible, coating them in chrome to make their substance dissolve in reflections. While the sculptural presence of his iconic 'Egg' and 'Swan' club chairs was intended to evoke a throne-like feel, Jacobsen took steps to counteract the chairs' mass. By fitting each with a single slender aluminium column anchored to a gleaming crisscross base, he created an unbroken line between the seat and the ground beneath it. The chairs were balancing acts of mass versus space, inviting the gaze to enjoy their curvaceous outlines from all angles.

ABOVE *Almost every Scandinavian home includes a few vintage pieces, with classics like Arne Jacobsen's 'Series 7' chairs, shown here, that may have been in the family for several generations. The teak sideboard was designed by Børge Mogensen, who created this model from straightforward, standardized components that could easily be constructed as a series rather than as a one-off design. Achille Castiglioni's 'Taccia' lamp has been popular in Denmark and Sweden since it was designed in 1962. It is pictured here alongside the fluted 'Arcus' vase, which was designed by Pia Törnell in 1995.*

ABOVE *The timelessness of contemporary Scandinavian furniture has enabled the Nordic interior to maintain the same distinctive look for nearly eighty years. By the 1930s, Alvar Aalto's bent-wood furniture displayed sleek, functionalist silhouettes. Aalto's sofa and chair, shown here in the same upholstery designs they would have had in the 1930s, are combined with contemporary Swedish designs: Katrin Hefner's 'KH1' floor lamp, Jonas Bohlin and Thomas Sandell's 'Snow' chests of drawers, and Mattias Ljunggren's 'Gute' chairs for Källemo.*

The high back of Jacobsen's 'Egg' chair arcs upwards in a protective enclosure that creates a sense of privacy. Its 'shell' is a single formation of seat, back and armrests that enables the person seated to remain upright in perfect comfort or to recline outstretched on the corresponding footstool. Each chair is designed to rotate on its base, turning to facilitate conversation or focus attention in another direction altogether. Jacobsen was a leading proponent of the open plan in his architectural designs, and conceiving chairs as enclosures helped to reinstate the sense of privacy sacrificed to the open space. When placed opposite each other, two 'Egg' chairs provide a sanctuary within a large space, while three or four can be grouped together to form a room of their own.

While Jacobsen's precise proportions were based on the trinity of the body, furniture and architecture, his fellow Dane Kaare Klint was one of the first designers to analyse and interrelate the proportions of the human body and the objects it sits on. The comfort of Klint's wood-and-leather 'Safari' chair of 1927 and his canework 'Deck Chair' of 1933 attests to the value of his research. Klint taught in the furniture faculty at the Royal Danish Academy of Fine Arts, where his scientific findings went on to shape the Danish Modern movement. Although Danish Modernism was based on principles of anatomy as well as functionalism, it also strived to create ideal proportions for all objects. Klint and his students, for example, meticulously recorded the number of pieces of cutlery in dinnerware sets and the measurements of each piece, to arrive at the ideal proportions for a dining-room sideboard.

The functionalist quest for perfect proportions led to a principle of standardization that specified the height of chair seats, the width of beds and the depth of drawers. Standards such as these constituted the backbone of the mass-produced industrial designs, and the concept of modular furniture. Mogens Koch, who had worked as an assistant to Klint, designed sectional furniture with corresponding tables and footstools. From the early 1950s to the '90s, Koch pioneered the refinement and standardization of 'ideal' forms.

The Swedish designer Bruno Mathsson's vision for modern, functional interiors was expressed in the minimalist furniture he designed in the 1930s and '40s. Mathsson's furniture was based on economy of design, replacing the heavy, formal styles of neoclassical furniture, which clashed with the clean lines and streamlined appearance of the modern home. His furniture designs were notable for a sleekness that integrated them into the modernist home like an architectural signature. At a time when ornamentation and trim were virtually banished from the interior, the hallmarks of interior carpentry found expression in the elegantly curved, dynamic lines of Mathsson's furniture.

Mathsson's first *Funkis* chair, the *'Gräshoppan',* or 'Grasshopper', was purchased for the reception area of a hospital in Värnamo. The design of the 'Grasshopper' stretched a woven-web seat across a frame whose armrests and legs were crafted from a single wooden piece sculpted into a curvaceous interpretation of a grasshopper's legs. The chair was spirited away to the attic after patients and staff at the hospital objected to its otherworldly shape. When the cobwebs were brushed off some sixty years later, the design appeared as sculptural and contemporary as when Mathsson had made it.

Mathsson's lounge chair 'Pernilla', on the other hand, became a resounding success throughout Scandinavia shortly after it debuted in 1944. Mathsson curved the legs and armrests dramatically to express a dynamic tension that makes 'Pernilla' seem ready to pounce. All of his furniture was designed to cradle the human body, creating optimal support as the person sat comfortably. Like Klint, Mathsson based his designs on anatomical studies, becoming one of the early pioneers of the scientific discipline known as ergonomics.

Mathsson's work drew upon many of the principles embodied in the furniture designs of Erik Gunnar Asplund. In the 1920s and '30s, Asplund designed lounge chairs and dining chairs with tubular steel frames, such as his chair for the Swedish Society for Industrial Design. A contemporary update of a side chair in the Biedermeier style (an early nineteenth-century furniture style popular in Germany, Austria and Scandinavia), the chair united space and clarity, simplicity and elegance in a timeless design.

Poul Henningsen perfected tubular steel in Denmark with his iconic 'Snake' chair of 1932, consisting of a single curved tube spiralled into a leather-covered seat and backrest.

Across the Baltic, in Finland, Alvar Aalto collaborated with his wife, Aino, to soften what many critics described as the 'harsh lines' of the modern home. Aalto coaxed plywood into new shapes to create simple, lightweight furniture in 'S' silhouettes or reclining contours that arced backwards dramatically. Many of his chairs and sofas were cantilevered on two plywood legs as though floating in mid-air – this conveyed a sense of movement and transparency, mirroring the principles of modernist architecture. By injecting fluid forms and natural materials into the interior, Aalto made the modern home seem anything but 'harsh'.

In 1932, Aalto designed one of the first flexible pieces of furniture ever made. The 'Aalto' sofa was crafted in tubular steel with a backrest that could be tilted backwards into a reclining slant or lowered into a horizontal position to transform the sofa into a bed. The divan introduced a notion of comfort and multi-functionality that could also change the role of the room around it. Although the 'Aalto' sofa is not in production today, the principles it conveyed survive in contemporary sofa beds and daybeds.

Josef Frank began designing furniture for the Swedish interior design company Svenskt Tenn in the early 1930s, moving to Stockholm from his native Austria to eventually become the chief designer. Frank designed numerous chairs, sofas and cupboards, taking inspiration from the nineteenth-century Arts and Crafts movement in Britain and *fin-de-siècle* Viennese designs. For much of his life, Frank remained true to the traditional Biedermeier idea that the home is a haven for leisure and luxury rather than efficiency and practicality. While Frank's works were based on a purity of form that captured the essence of Nordic Modernism, they were given a luxurious feel by exquisite craftsmanship and high-quality materials. Frank excelled as a cabinetmaker, designing elegant cabinets and cunning chests of drawers in walnut and mahogany rather than Scandinavian elm and birch. He set these atop wooden stands to make them appear as lightweight as possible, intending to make rooms seem more open and spacious. Frank's key furniture designs continue to be manufactured and sold by Svenskt Tenn today, and many have been in continuous production since the 1930s.

The Danish designer Finn Juhl pioneered floating forms, and his furniture designs are remarkable for the sheer virtuosity of their craftsmanship. Juhl's 'Chieftain' chair, designed in 1949, featured a low-slung seat and tapering back that peaked into horn-like configurations in each corner. The armrests spilled over the frame in undulating curves

RIGHT *In Scandinavia, it is not unusual to find homes that are almost entirely furnished with Josef Frank's designs. Frank's work was distinctively modern, yet the antithesis of the functionalistic furniture of his contemporaries in Sweden. At a time when motifs and decorative details virtually disappeared in Scandinavia, Frank's work celebrated lavish patterns and rich textures. He appliquéd vintage botanical illustrations to this mahogany chest, and crafted backrests for these cherry-wood chairs by binding rattan ribs to their polished frames. Here, they flank Frank's '771' dining table, also in cherry wood.*

BELOW *Hans Wegner's 'Wishbone' Chair from 1950 recalls the elegant lines of the classical Ming furniture produced in fourteenth-century China. Throughout his career, Wegner's works expressed a deep appreciation for the materials and craftsmanship of the Far East, and the philosophies behind them.*

that recalled organic shapes. Although Juhl worked with a wide range of woods, teak was his material of choice, and he developed a number of techniques specifically for its use. Juhl's influence led to the widespread use of teak in modern Scandinavian furniture, contributing to the Danish 'Teak' style of the 1950s.

Juhl's wooden chests, cabinets and shelving units either had fixtures that anchored them to the wall and cantilevered them over the floor, or were set several feet (120 centimetres) above the ground atop a wooden base that allowed them to clear skirting boards (baseboards) and stand flush against the wall. Like Frank's mahogany cabinets, Juhl's Oregon pine sideboard of 1953 featured small drawers in a variety of sizes and was supported by a frame rather than being secured to legs. The sideboard appeared to float within the frame that surrounded it, giving the effect of two separate pieces crafted in different styles.

Juhl's designs reflected the fluid abstractions of sculptors such as Hans Arp and Alexander Calder, whose rotating forms inspired Juhl to express movement in furniture. Seminal pieces, such as his 1940 upholstered sofa for the furniture manufacturer Niels Vodder and his 1940 'Pelican' chair, were radically different from the modernist reworkings of classical furniture designs. Juhl's furniture took on surreal characteristics as he created a floating effect by cantilevering the body over the legs, and crafted the backrests of sofas into shapes resembling the wingspan of a bird in flight. Armrests took the shape of camel humps, or were effaced into gentle curves. Many of Juhl's sofas separated the backrest entirely from the seat, curving them instead into similar, yet individual, concave shapes that bring to mind an upholstered, open clamshell.

A cabinetmaking contemporary of Juhl, the Danish designer Nanna Ditzel shared his vision of designing to ideal scales. One of the few women to compete in the male-dominated arena of modern furniture design, Ditzel gained recognition for her comfortable, unassuming pieces. In the 1950s, Ditzel and her husband, Jørgen, designed a series of small-scale, solid-wood stools (called 'Toadstools') and a high chair for children, to give them an ergonomically friendly environment. Leather flaps and laces were used in all the places that would normally have required screws and hinges. In the following decade, Ditzel began designing asymmetrical forms and sensuous, flowing motifs, providing a chic antidote to the minimalism associated with Scandinavian furniture.

The Danish designer Hans Wegner began his career as a cabinet-maker in the late 1920s, going on to work with Arne Jacobsen during the war years. In 1946, he teamed up with the minimalistic furniture designer Børge Mogensen, and the two of them carved a niche for furniture craftsmanship that led to its being recognized as a discipline in its own right. Most furniture-makers were either master cabinetmakers who constructed furniture according to time-honoured methods, or modernist architects who designed furniture as a sideline. Wegner and Mogensen were among the first generation in Denmark to be called *formgivar*, which translates as 'designer'.

Wegner's wooden chairs were distinguished by their elegant lines and ability to balance formal characteristics with functionalistic ease. His *'Runde Stol'*, or 'Round Chair', of 1949 was based on Ming Dynasty elegance to merge the armrests and back gracefully into one another. Wegner introduced a number of innovations that have inspired designers around the world: the jacket chair 'Valet' had a backrest crafted in the shape of a coat hanger; the folding 'PP 512' chair could be hung on the wall to be stored out of the way; and the *'Cirkel'* easy chair had casters fitted to the back legs, with the front legs designed as handles to enable the chair to be manoeuvred like a wheelbarrow.

From the late 1940s onwards, furniture began to move from the floor to the wall, as wall-mounted furnishings grew in popularity. In Sweden, the 'String' shelving system designed by Nisse Strinning in 1949 became a staple item of almost every *Funkis* home. Crafted in mahogany and steel coated in PVC (vinyl), 'String' was an extensive modular system designed to 'modernize' any home instantly, as it provided wall space for storage, display, lighting and desk sets. 'String' incorporated several different types of furniture into its design, reducing the number of individual pieces needed in the household and making efficient use of the space. Conscious that its sleek surfaces would be used for display, Strinning chose wood veneer with a luminous sheen that would enhance the objects placed upon it. The 'String' system transformed the way that shelves and side tables were used, by making it clear that they were no longer repositories where objects could be dumped indiscriminately. Although 'String' eventually went out of production, it enjoyed a revival in the 1990s that brought it out of second-hand shops and into auction rooms.

The Danish designer Poul Kjaerholm's flawless furniture of the 1960s has never dated, which is probably why he is counted among the greatest Scandinavian furniture designers. Kjaerholm was some twenty years younger than Arne Jacobsen and his contemporaries, and his work exemplified a second wave of Danish design that found expression in strips of dynamic steel and metallic grids rather than bent plywood. Kjaerholm often combined a steel frame with fabric upholstery, leather or canework, as in his sweeping 'PK 24' lounge chair. His 'PK 80' daybed became an icon of contemporary cool, revealing strong parallels with the brand of modernism pioneered by Mies van der Rohe and Le Corbusier. Kjaerholm's 'PK 61' coffee table tops a steel frame with glass, through which the staggered legs are visible. The design is succinct and austere, but captivating in its geometric simplicity. It is a table that has nothing to hide, but much to say – its balancing of sculptural form with everyday function embodies the concept that less is more.

ABOVE *Poul Henningsen's '4-shade' enamel pendant lamp was designed in 1926, but has proved to be even more popular today than it was when Louis Poulsen first manufactured it. Here, the arcing curves of Henningsen's lamp echo the rounded backs of dining chairs designed by Nanna Ditzel.*

Style revolution

As the style rebellion of the 1960s swept through Scandinavia, furniture designers reacted against the strict functionalism of the 1930s, '40s and '50s to capture the essence of the youth revolution. Characterized for decades by its cool minimalism and understated elegance, Scandinavian furniture suddenly took on funky, colourful and even erotic undertones. Many of the designs produced at this time were meant to be seen as metaphors rather than just as furniture, while others simply looked too good to use.

By this time, Scandinavian furniture was being influenced by new materials and new moulding techniques, and designed in shapes that were more forgiving and more closely associated with relaxation than comfort. Because their malleable properties enabled them to bend and contort into shapes that wood could not achieve, fibreglass, plastics and aluminium were rivalling the natural materials that had prevailed for centuries. While these man-made materials opened up a whole new spectrum of possibilities, Scandinavian designers remained true to the principle that designs should be durable, functional and sustainable.

The visionary Danish designer Verner Panton crafted chairs, tables and light fittings in plastic, introducing a rainbow of saturated colours and space-age forms that would radically change design techniques. Panton took inspiration from spatial geometry to create his series of 'Cone' chairs in wire, which he upholstered in bold primary colours. Merging ideas of sitting, lying and reclining, Panton designed his 'Peacock T5' chair of 1960 as a round wire basket lined with cushions to nestle into. By offering an alternative to sitting in a formal upright posture, Panton was equating furniture with the type of relaxation promoted by the new 'lounge' lifestyle.

Exhibiting his work at a contemporary furniture fair, Panton hung his 'Cone' chair upside down from the ceiling so that its geometrical shape could be appreciated. His ubiquitous 'Panton' chair, a dramatic wave that sweeps upwards from the floor and dips into a contoured seat and rounded backrest, was crafted in dense plastic. It has never wavered in appeal since it was designed in 1960, and continues to make an artistic statement decades later. Panton's minimalist forms and svelte shapes set a benchmark in Scandinavian design, and they also started a craze for 'space-age' furniture around the world.

A fellow Dane, Steen Østergaard, had trained in the design consultancy of Finn Juhl but followed the single-form, single-material plastic shapes pioneered by Panton. Østergaard, like Panton, cantilevered chair seats over their bases, but with scooped-out lower sections and deeper backrests. Whereas Panton's sweeping forms were conceived as a seamless flow of surfaces, Østergaard fitted seat cushions into the plastic frames to contrast soft textures with the glossy sheen of plastic. Each piece was lightweight and easy to pick up and move, meaning that handling became an important feature of the furniture. This introduced an erotic element to the allure of the furniture, which many other designers have since factored into the appeal of their work.

BELOW *Originally borrowed from yacht-makers, fibreglass became the material of choice for many Scandinavian designers in the 1960s and '70s. Along with reinforced plastic and elasticated upholstery, it enabled them to rebel against the rectilinearity of wooden furniture and design curvaceous chairs like these.*

THIS PAGE *Eero Saarinen was the son of the celebrated Finnish architect Eliel Saarinen and his textile designer wife, Loja. Born in Helsinki, Eero emigrated with his family to the United States in 1923, where he produced many highly successful furniture designs. His 'Tulip' table and chairs balanced their mass atop a pedestal base, eschewing the norm of four-legged structures. The floor lamp to the left is one of Alvar Aalto's lighting designs, while the white opaline pendant light was designed by Yki Nummi in 1963.*

The craze for space-age furniture spread to Iceland, where designers contributed with shapes that were streamlined and sculptural. Sections from NASA's Saturn V rocket inspired Gunnar Magnússon's 'Apollo' chair of 1967, while the bubbles of Buckminster Fuller's geodesic domes influenced the design of Einar Þorsteinn Ásgeirsson's 'Bucky' chair. Both designers drew upon geometric shapes and smooth planes to arrive at sleek, visionary forms.

One of several designers to place Finnish furniture on an international platform during the 1960s, Eero Aarnio began working with fibreglass to create a range of arresting new forms. The arcing silhouettes and undulating contours of Aarnio's work are more often likened to the sensual curves of Henry Moore's sculptures than to traditional furniture. Aarnio's best-known series of designs from this period include his womb-like 'Ball' or 'Globe' chair from 1962, and his low, lateral 'Pastilli' chair from 1967. Aarnio's pedestal armchair for the Finnish furniture company Asko, the seat of which appears to be scooped out of a fibreglass orb, suggests a snug cocoon to curl up in rather than a conventional seat. Aarnio gave transparency full reign in his hanging 'Bubble' chair, a cult favourite he designed in 1968 to give the illusion of floating in mid-air.

Also Finnish, Yrjö Kukkapuro anchored his furniture designs firmly to the ground with amoeba-like feet and sleigh-like runners of tubular steel. Kukkapuro believed that a comfortable chair should be a negative relief of the human form. To make his world-famous 'Karuselli', or 'Carousel', chair of 1965, he moulded wire mesh into the form of his own seated body, which he attached to a tubular metal frame to create a single-form shell seat.

BELOW LEFT Eero Aarnio's 'Globe' chair was designed in 1962, creating a womb-like enclosure that provided a sense of refuge in a hectic environment.
BELOW Poul Volther designed his 'Corona' chair in 1961. In it he expanded his interpretation of the classic ladder-back chair that he had explored in earlier teak designs (see page 123), as this detail reveals.

The Norwegian designer Terje Ekstrøm also took the seated human form as the basis of his furniture, but he pioneered ergonomic designs that would continue to support the back as the sitter assumed a range of different postures. Ekstrøm's *'Ekstrem'*, or 'Extreme', chair, designed in 1984, bends a number of tube-shaped components into voluptuous curves that take on the abstraction of sculpture more than the familiar shape of furniture. Furniture designers and artists alike regarded the chair as an interactive sculpture, and Ekstrøm's 'Extreme' chair became a seminal design that inspired other Scandinavian furniture designers to accommodate the movements of the human body.

Grete Jalk, a Swedish-born designer who trained with Kaare Klint in Copenhagen, won awards for the perfect sculptural balance of the teak-faced laminate plywood chair and accompanying nest of tables that she designed in 1963. Considered to be both a work of art and a piece of fine furniture, the chair featured curves with small radii that bent the wood practically to breaking point. The breathtaking design recalled the folds of draped fabric more than it did moulded plywood. The accompanying nest of tables interlocked into a tripod – each one was constructed with the same radical curves as the chair, and the table-top folded into the legs it rested on.

In the 1960s, a younger crop of Danish designers rebelled against the emerging 'Teak' style that signalled a classical undercurrent in Danish furniture. Aagaard Andersen, an artist who experimented with furniture, worked with foam and fibreglass to create unpredictable, organic designs. His work established a 'bohemian' furniture culture a world apart from the refined shapes that had characterized Scandinavian furniture for several decades.

Sculptural form

In Scandinavia today, a new generation of designers are interpreting furniture as sculptural forms, treating functionality as a basis for aesthetic expression. Danish designers are leading the pack with their exchanges between contemporary art, architecture and design, in a range of highly imaginative furniture so sculptural that utility does not appear to be the first consideration. Often, traditional materials are combined with new design technologies to present fresh visions of how furniture design will unfold in the future.

Torben Quaade uses new techniques to manipulate organic materials, spiralling wooden slats into a chair shape resembling an inverted snail shell. Sebastian Holmbäck uses thermoplastic techniques to produce works from a single piece of plastic with the same considerations that a sculptor would have when chiselling a piece of stone.

Based in London, the Danish designer Mathias Bengtsson makes sculptural furniture that is both visually arresting and technically innovative. Bengtsson works with principles of simplicity and transparency to craft furniture in floating parallel lines and sculptural shapes. His 'Slice' chairs and *chaises longues* were designed through computer-mapping techniques and constructed from layers of aluminium, plywood or Perspex (Plexiglas) cut with laser precision. The 'Slice' series was constructed with the adeptness of an architect creating a topological map of the landscape, achieving the illusion of a piece of furniture cut away from a cliff face and scaled to human proportions.

While 'Slice' chairs are given their unique shape by separating layers of material to create a semi-translucent structure, the modular layers of Bengtsson's 'Modular Aluminium Concept' bench (the 'MAC' bench) soften extruded chrome-coated aluminium into sculptural contours that melt away the hard angles of conventional furniture. The finish of the 'MAC' bench is polished to a high gloss that gives an impression of depth beneath its surface, as though the furniture were slowly dissolving.

Bengtsson has also received much acclaim for his collection of spun carbon-fibre *chaises longues*. The feather-light, semi-transparent structure of the *chaise* belies the extraordinary strength of the carbon. Bengtsson spins one continuous carbon thread which is woven into a slender, mesh-like surface forming a cylindrical shape. The flexibility of the mesh moulds to the body and cradles the sitter in the same comfort that would be afforded by a sprung base. In his uncompromising search for a visionary expression, Bengtsson appears to have discovered a direction so promising that it could portend the furniture of the future.

Sven Lundh, the visionary behind the Swedish furniture manufacturer Källemo, resolved to move away from traditional forms by commissioning furniture from artists and sculptors. Inspired by the concepts behind Marcel Duchamp's 'ready-mades' (randomly chosen manufactured objects presented as artworks) and the art–furniture hybrids created by Donald Judd, Lundh spotted the potential to inject furniture with principles of fine art. He discovered Jonas Bohlin's 'Concrete' chair, a tubular-steel and concrete construction that had been made for Bohlin's degree show at Konstfack art school in Stockholm, which he manufactured at Källemo in 1982. Ten years later, Källemo presented Mats Theselius's darkly erotic '*Chaise Longue*', a sinister interpretation of a classical icon in black leather padding and black wooden cladding with visible brass screws. Today, Källemo is continuing

LEFT *Antti Nurmesniemi's 'Model No. 001' chaise longue was designed in 1968 and upholstered in one of the graphic 'Piccolo' textiles designed by his wife, Vuokko. The* chaise *radically reverses the position traditionally assumed by the reclining body, elevating the legs and feet to chest height by lowering the seat to just above floor level. The wooden screen is by Poul Kjærholm.*

to produce limited editions of furniture commissioned from designers and artists, forging a new era of design as they blur the boundaries between furniture and art.

Generating a resurgence of interest in Norwegian contemporary furniture, the Oslo-based design cooperative Norway Says was formed with state sponsorship and has since brought acclaim to Norwegian furniture design as well as interior design. Acknowledging that Norwegian furniture was typically described as 'cabin-looking', Andreas Engesvik, Torbjørn Anderssen, Tore Borgersen and Espen Voll joined forces to design everyday furniture in sleek shapes that speak of artistic elan and minimalistic architecture. Each trained in furniture design and interior architecture at Norway's National University of Art and Design.

Andreas Engesvik's forward-thinking designs are often characterized by smooth surfaces that sweep upwards rather than terminating in a level edge. The top surface of his 'Alto' writing desk resembles a three-sided tray balanced atop two free-standing steel frames that provide stable support without interconnecting underneath the writing surface. His padded armchair, 'Frank', is also crafted in bent wood, with arms drawn upwards to the same height as the back to provide a nest-like environment for those seated. Neither 'Alto' nor 'Frank' is constructed with conventional edges. Corners are negated as surfaces are contoured into a continuous sweep or cut away altogether.

Espen Voll's 'Hole' table transformed a two-wheeled upright trolley into a coffee-table shape, morphing its wheels and handles into four legs and its frame into a smooth table-top. The 'Hole' table combines the function of a level surface with pop-art sensibilities, revealing that a table can be a work of art in itself. Collaborating with Bjørn Bye from the Norwegian design group K8, Voll designed the '360' chair, which reinvents the office swivel chair for the home milieu in an elegant design that is too spectacular to hide behind a desk.

Former Norway Says member Frode Myhr has established his own studio in Bergen. Myhr's 'Name' *chaise* bends a single upholstered plane into a sweeping surface designed to cradle the body from head to toe, set atop two sleigh-like runners. While Norway once had a reputation for lagging behind its neighbours in furniture design, the combined efforts of Norway Says and Frode Myhr are taking Norwegian furniture in an exciting new direction.

ABOVE *The Oslo-based design cooperative Norway Says is creating a distinctive identity for contemporary Norwegian design. Torbjørn Anderssen's 'Paper Master' magazine holder (far left) bends plywood nearly to breaking point to create these tight angles. This stackable chair by Norwegian designers Fredrik and Solveig Torsteinsen (centre) is elegant but remarkably lightweight. The design combines a thin slice of laminated wood with a slender steel frame. Espen Voll and Tore Borgersen's 'Pancras' chair (above) merges an upholstered seat with a curving support, balanced weightlessly atop a sleek metal frame.*

RIGHT *Arne Jacobsen moulded plywood into flowing lines whose surfaces assumed organic contours almost impossible to achieve in dense hardwoods. Here, Jacobsen's 'Grand Prix' chairs from 1955 are grouped round the 'Superellipsis' table designed by Piet Hein and Bruno Mathsson in 1964.*

ESSENTIAL
DETAILS

ESSENTIAL DETAILS The beauty of nature has exerted a strong influence over the decorative styles of the Scandinavian countries for many centuries. Design traditions have long been characterized by a wide range of visual symbols and organic forms that directly reflect the enjoyment of the beautiful Nordic landscape.

Nature has often been an important inspiration for Nordic craftsmanship, art and design. Materials from the natural world, such as metal, wood and clay, provide a rich harvest of untainted colours and original forms, while elements of nature also find expression in the patterns and motifs adorning glass, ceramics and textiles. Furniture remains the showpiece of Scandinavian design, but many other objects are equally seductive in their appeal. Wood, metal and clay – indigenous to the Nordic landscape – remain the materials of choice among Scandinavian craftsmen today, despite the availability of high-quality synthetic alternatives. As ancient craft skills are married to modern design practice, the use of traditional techniques and natural materials gives contemporary designs a human touch.

For centuries, textile fibres have been harvested and spun into a range of woven fabrics. Scandinavian textiles have many associations: sensuous, decorative, functional, ritual. While the earliest textiles provided a source of comfort, warmth and protection, they also reflected styles and techniques that crossed borders or defined cultural boundaries. They were stitched and embroidered with motifs that attest to a strong heritage of storytelling and symbolism, or printed with patterns and images that also excite the senses and evoke memories. Nordic textiles have always been as varied as the landscapes they came from, and modern-day designers are breaking new ground as they combine traditional forms with unconventional influences in contemporary styles.

The term 'tradition' often seems the opposite of 'modern' and the enduring qualities of the values of the past. But the use of traditional materials today retraces a path already travelled, implying a continuous flow of skills and appreciation of techniques that anchor modern objects in the splendours of the past. In the hands of Scandinavian designers, the reverence for wood, ceramic, glass, metalware and textiles is a constant renewal of those principles.

A survey of Scandinavia's contemporary designs would be incomplete without a closer look at the traditional crafts and skills that have inspired their purity of form. The classic techniques viewed as craft traditions in many parts of the world are recognized as disciplines of the arts in Scandinavia, fine arts that allow creative inspiration to be communicated with the hands. While all the materials can be used to manufacture functional objects that speak of streamlined utility, they are also crafted into works of art that transcend their function and meaning. Today's designers, irrespective of their choice of media, are driven by artistic sentiments as they find fresh expressions for time-honoured craft traditions.

ABOVE *While furniture is often considered to be the interior's defining feature, fine objects made in ceramic, glass, metal or wood provide the vital essence we interpret as 'style'. Textiles, colours and motifs establish a voice of their own; as they energize the home or create a subdued feel, they prove that details make all the difference.* **RIGHT** *Natural motifs play an important role in decoration.*

A ANNUA L.

PILBLAD, SAGITTARIA SAGITTIFOLIA L.

STIÄRNTISTEL, CARLINA VULGARIS L.

SVALTING ALISMA

AGO FARFARA L.

VASS, PHRAGMITES COMMUNIS TRIN.

A. PRAKTNEJLIKA, DIANTHUS SUPERBUS L.

GRANBRÄKEN, ASPID

Ceramics

The Scandinavian countries trace the history of their ceramics back to the Vikings and beyond, when early potters learned to transform the basic elements of fire, earth, air and water into objects that were both beautiful and functional. These early designs were works of distinction, growing more refined over the years as craftsmen balanced their esoteric and aesthetic features against their functional uses. That said, for many centuries the Nordic countries lagged behind the rest of Europe, relying on imports of fine porcelain from Europe and the Far East before producing their own porcelain in the seventeenth century.

The establishment of state-supported kilns in Sweden and Denmark enabled domestic markets to flourish and generated a demand for Scandinavian ceramics abroad. Rörstrand, in Sweden, was founded by government charter in 1726 to manufacture blue-and-white faience, fine porcelain and functional earthenware vessels. At the end of the eighteenth century, Rörstrand adopted a so-called 'English' style of cream-coloured earthenware known as *Flint-porslin*, and emulated many of the popular English motifs. The demand for Rörstrand's goods in the Baltic countries led to the founding of its sister company Arabia, in Helsinki, in 1873, to produce ceramics for the Russian market.

BELOW *For a long time, ceramics had less artistic kudos than painting or sculpture, but their unique beauty can have the same impact on the interior. The simple forms of Berndt Friberg's stoneware vases introduced an influential style that shaped studio ceramics throughout the 1950s and '60s.*

The Gustavsberg kilns were established nearly a hundred years after Rörstrand was founded, in a former brickworks site on the island of Värmdö outside Stockholm. Gustavsberg, too, was influenced by British kilns, importing clay from England and employing British craftsmen to produce transfer-print designs or hand-painted floral motifs.

The Royal Copenhagen porcelain factory gained royal patronage in 1779, when the Danish king intervened to save a fledgling kiln from bankruptcy. He incorporated the factory into his scheme for transforming Denmark into a cultural centre, planning to export its wares to the other courts of Europe. The king commissioned the factory to produce a multicoloured, rococo style known as the '*Flora Danica*', or 'Danish Flowers', service in 1789, intended for presentation to the court of Catherine the Great of Russia. Each of the flowers was chosen from a botanical catalogue of Danish flora, and painted single-handedly by a sole artist. The service was not completed until 1802, when it numbered a staggering total of 1,802 pieces. Ultimately, the set was so beautiful that it was retained by the Danish king, who refused to part with it.

In Norway, the Porsgrund porcelain factory was established in 1886, at Porsgrunn, near Oslo, and for many years reproduced the transfer-printed designs that had originated in the Royal Copenhagen factory and the Meissen factory in Germany. As the Nordic revival styles took hold and the National Romanticism movement formed at the end of the nineteenth century, Porsgrund began to produce its own Nordic patterns. The motifs mirrored the nationalistic sentiments that motivated Norway to declare its independence from Sweden in 1905. The artists Henrik Bull and Gerhard Munthe produced neo-Viking designs based on ancient intertwined motifs and hybrid animal forms.

LEFT *The delicate shapes of ceramics by the Swedish painter Ingela Hedlund Claxton are emphasized by understated textures and organic contours. Her lateral pieces, like the one shown here, are fragile landscapes as much as they are exuberant abstractions. A streak of colour may represent the flow of water,* *while a textured surface maps out the surrounding terrain.*
BELOW *Wilhelm Kåge excelled as a painter before joining Gustavsberg as artistic director in 1917. His artistic sensibilities found full expression in ceramic designs such as these, charting the shift from the functionalism of the 1920s to the modernism of the 1950s.*

In the early years of the twentieth century, the art nouveau style swept through the far north, with Rörstrand becoming the first Swedish kiln to express the style, in a number of vases and platters characterized by relief decoration of relatively large, sweeping, stylized flowers and trailing leaves. The use of subtle modelling and figurative techniques enabled Rörstrand to produce a range of porcelain collectables, such as figures of birds and animals and art nouveau figurines. The art nouveau style was mastered in Denmark by Thorvald Bindesbøll, the leading designer of his generation, whose work influenced many other Scandinavian designers. Bindesbøll's trademark simplicity and abstract motifs seemed to anticipate the modernist movement to come.

When Nora Gulbrandsen became the Porsgrund's artistic director in 1928, she introduced bold geometric repeats in orange, black, ochre and sky blue. Gulbrandsen's motifs were inspired by the work of the Russian avant-gardists and the influential Wiener Werkstätte in Austria. Tias Eckhoff followed her as artistic director, designing award-winning ranges that brought overdue recognition to Norwegian ceramics. Eckhoff's '*Det Riflede*', or 'Fluted', set won a gold medal at the Milan Triennale exhibition in 1954, while his '*Glohane*', or 'Gazing', range won a gold medal at the event four years later.

In Sweden, Gustavsberg changed tactics dramatically in the 1920s as the *Svenska Slöjdförening* – Swedish Craft Association – lobbied industrialists to entrust artistic direction to artists rather than to craftsmen. Responding to the social reformer Ellen Key's appeal for more beautiful objects to be made in everyday life, the state promoted an alliance between art and industry to improve the design of everyday objects and make beauty as important as function.

The 1930 Stockholm Exhibition marked a turning point in Swedish design, with the *Funkis* movement impacting upon ceramics as well as furniture. Wilhelm Kåge's *Funkis*-style ceramics represented Gustavsberg at the exhibition, where his austerely minimal '*Pyro*' range received critical acclaim. '*Pyro*' was among the first sets of ceramics to be used as both cooking utensils and a dining set. The pieces could be purchased individually rather than as a complete set, which made them more affordable to a broader range of people. Kåge set another example for functionalistic ceramics with his 1933 '*Praktika*' earthenware range, which he graded into sizes that could nest inside each other for easy storage, or stack together for efficient use.

Kåge managed to shake off his shrewd sense of design economy from time to time and design sculptural pieces. Taking inspiration from surrealism and cubism, he also created hybrid forms and organic shapes that seemed to fragment into obtuse angles. The voluptuous contours of '*Våga*', his range of white stoneware vessels, seemed to melt into delicately fluted rims, while his moulded stoneware '*Farsta*' pieces resembled beanpod-like organic forms. Kåge was also inspired by ceramic shapes from Mexico and the Far East.

LEFT *Scandinavian ceramics came into their own during the mid-twentieth century, when artistic pieces became more expressive and, at the same time, functional objects were radically streamlined, as the varied selection pictured here demonstrates.*

BELOW *The unwavering popularity of Stig Lindberg's ceramics attests to his mastery of form and motif. His elliptical shapes gave poetic expression to functional ceramics, while his folk-inspired earthenware, like this colourful vase, was warm and whimsical.*

As the functionalist movement began to influence Finnish ceramics, the Finnish pottery factory Arabia appointed Kurt Ekholm to establish an art department in 1932, premised on streamlined functionalistic designs. Ekholm had studied in Sweden and returned to Finland with a sense of elegant utility that found expression in designs well suited to mass production. Ekholm's celebrated 'Sinivalko', or 'Blue and White', service exemplified his commitment to Funkis principles. Its simple banded decorations, stackable pieces and inexpensive production costs proclaimed Ellen Key's manifesto for a good design for all.

Kaj Franck became director of the design studio at Arabia in 1945, introducing the revolutionary 'Kilta', or 'Guild', range of heat-resistant earthenware in 1948. In 1957, Ulla Procopé, Franck's colleague, designed the innovative 'Liekki', or 'Flame', covered dishes, the lids of which doubled as serving dishes. Procopé introduced a hand-crafted quality to Arabia's mass-produced designs by applying a mottled brown glaze to the 'Ruska', or 'Autumn', series of 1960, bestowing the effect of hand-thrown ceramics.

At Gustavsberg, Stig Lindberg had trained under Kåge before taking over from him as artistic director in 1949. Lindberg took an organic approach to ceramics that found expression in simple lines and bold contours reminiscent of the art deco style. By the post-war era, his designs were acknowledged as prime examples of Scandinavian modernism. Lindberg's elliptical forms had an organic elegance previously unseen in Nordic ceramics. His bold forms were virtually devoid of integral ornamentation, and were designed in asymmetrical shapes sparingly decorated with motifs inspired by traditional folk symbols.

Tapio Wirkkala, one of the leading figures in twentieth-century Finnish design, worked across a range of disciplines. His ceramic designs ranged from the mundanity of functional objects to highly exclusive, individual pieces that often blurred the boundaries between art and design. Wirkkala was commissioned by the Swedish pottery factory Rosenthal to produce a variety of ceramic designs in the 1970s. His 'Pollo' vases of 1970 were sublimely contoured abstractions cast in quasi-elliptical forms that Wirkkala smoothed into a blunted point. Wirkkala moved from abstraction to pop art in 1977, inventing a white ceramic version of a crumpled paper bag.

Today, Scandinavian ceramicists are renowned throughout the world for their innovative designs and synthesis of artistic disciplines. Many designers work in several different media, such as glass and metalwork, to create designs that lend themselves to a variety of materials. The Swedish furniture designer Jonas Bohlin undertook a commission by Rörstrand in 2000, resulting in a range of understated porcelain tableware known as the 'Qvint' set. Pia Törnell designed her 'Arcus' vase for Rörstrand in 1995, followed by her wood-and-ceramic 'Grade' tableware of 2000. Arabia has also manufactured ranges produced by furniture designers, appointing Stefan Lindfors and Harri Koskinen as creative directors in recent years.

Ingegerd Råman, one of Sweden's leading glass designers, also designs ceramics for Gustavsberg, while the artist Åsa Lindström grafts vintage black-and-white photographs of men and women dancing onto the surfaces of her ceramics to add a surrealist effect. The Swedish painter Ingela Hedlund Claxton applies her brush strokes to ceramic contours with the same sensitivity she shows to her canvases, and has been distinguished by her studio ranges of rustic shapes, lacework motifs and sweeping abstractions.

RIGHT *Drawn in simple lines and coloured with muted pastels, Stig Lindberg's distinctive leaf motifs became a hallmark of his style. Lindberg preferred natural forms and figurative motifs to geometric designs and radical abstractions, which he drew freehand or painted with swift brush strokes. Throughout his forty-year career, Lindberg developed a distinctive pictorial vocabulary that gave his work a unique artistic quality.*

Glassware

By the mid-twentieth century, Scandinavian glass had come of age. Artists had replaced craftsmen as glass designers, and simplicity had been acknowledged as a principle of beauty and refinement. Ironically, the *Funkis* drive towards utility led to a greater appreciation of glass as a time-honoured art form. As glassworks streamlined their main lines of vases, cooking vessels, tumblers and wine glasses, the workrooms were divided into studios for creating art glass and workshops for developing mass-produced ranges. Bold designs in both departments revealed a new sculptural confidence that was beginning to emerge in Scandinavian glass, and went on to revolutionize the production of everyday glass utensils.

With glass once more becoming a field for artistry and innovation, designers experimented with new techniques, the effects of original colour pigments and the use of different additives. At the Orrefors glassworks in Sweden, founded in 1898, the creative direction had been in the hands of four young designers – Edvin Öhrström, Nils Landberg, Sven Palmqvist and Ingeborg Lundin – since 1944. They devised techniques and colours that revolutionized the industry, creating designs that appeared to be sculpted with water, painted with colour and glowing with an inner light. Their use of dense glass and deeply cut geometric motifs explored the optical and reflective qualities of the medium, while giving their designs a multi-faceted, jewel-like quality.

Orrefors had gained a reputation for artistic innovation during the 1920s, when Edward Hald and Simon Gate began designing modernist glassware. Hald's etched and engraved pieces drew stylistic references from Matisse, while his economical pressed-glass designs retained their artistic integrity despite being mass-produced. Likewise, Gate was one of the first glass designers to treat glass as an art form, setting a standard for virtuosity and innovation that has been upheld by following generations of glass artists.

Sven Palmqvist had begun to explore the possibilities of coloured glass in the 1930s, developing his *Kraka* technique of sandwiching grid-like patterns of coloured glass between clear layers on either side. During the late 1940s and '50s, he produced his 'Ravenna' ranges, inspired by the colours and configurations of the Byzantine mosaics he observed on a trip to Italy. Palmqvist suspended pieces of coloured glass in his forms to create a variegated mosaic effect. Edvin Öhrström also suspended his patterns within layers of glass, developing the Ariel technique of sandblasting motifs into a clear glass plate before folding it within molten glass in a way that formed pockets of air. In the 1950s, Öhrström's technique found full expression in his '*Vattenlek*', or 'Water Play', series, in designs that appeared to trap seaweed and sea creatures in glass as if they were still submerged under water.

Nils Landberg produced a series of abstract pattern designs engraved on shallow bowls and tulip-shaped vases, which led to a series of glasses with breathtakingly thin, exaggeratedly long stems. These '*Tulpan*', or 'Tulip', glasses of 1957 proved to be the most difficult designs the glass-blowers had ever attempted, but the beauty of their forms and the praise they received made their efforts well worthwhile.

Ingeborg Lundin was acclaimed in the 1950s and early '60s for her sculptural pieces of glassware. Rather than accepting the limitations of glass, Lundin maintained that she worked with the properties of light, transparency and radiant colour, which she captured

ABOVE FAR LEFT *Vicke Lindstrand is one of Sweden's most renowned glass artists, and his early style reflected his interests in cubism, constructivism and modernism. By the 1950s, his work had shifted away from such formalist idioms to poetic expressions of the landscape, as his 'Winter' vase from around 1953 illustrates.*

ABOVE LEFT *For more than two centuries, Orrefors glassworks in Sweden has excelled at designing beautiful decanters.*

LEFT *Kjell Engman's set of 'Macho' decanters for Kosta Boda renders a whimsical abstraction of three young men striking confident poses.*

157

in her celebrated glass forms. Her acclaimed '*Äpple*', or 'Apple', vase of 1955 was an outstanding example of her ability to capture the beauty of an everyday object in glass, changing for ever the way her generation saw the ordinary apple.

Founded in 1742, Kosta Boda is Sweden's longest-surviving glassworks, but one that often lagged behind Orrefors in its modernist designs for the twentieth century. When Vicke Lindstrand became its artistic director in 1950, he brought with him several of the techniques he had developed while working for Orrefors throughout the 1930s and '40s. But he pushed forward with such innovations as his 1957 '*Träd Dimma*', or 'Trees in the Fog', vase, which drew the stark outlines of birch branches amid the misty white tints of the vase. His 'Negress' vase of 1953 elongated the shape of a Ndebele tribeswoman's neck and head, crafting the base in the shape of her *zila* necklaces, which rounded into the contours of her face before stretching into the tight curls of her coiffure. Lindstrand transformed the company's output into some of the most expressive sculptural glassworks of his time.

Lindstrand found a rival in the Norwegian glass artist Willy Johansson, who became the head of the design team at Hadeland glassworks in 1958. Johansson took responsibility for

the artistic direction of Hadeland's studio while also overseeing the production of the pressed glassware produced in the factory. Johansson's free-blown designs were remarkably restrained, and he often achieved a near-perfect symmetry in their shapes. His coloured glassware gradually intensified as the colours were drawn towards the outer edges, which Johansson bordered with his signature opaque rims. He was awarded the *Diplôme d'Honneur* at the Milan Triennale in 1954 for his ground-breaking designs, including the sandblasted vases he blew into wooden moulds and gave cores of contrasting colours.

Per Lütken, the artistic director of Holmegaard, the Danish glassworks, drew upon the company's traditional principles of simplicity, classical form and high quality to design its first ranges of modern glass in the 1950s. Lütken reinvented classical standards like the wine glass, shifting its mass around the stem and blowing an air bubble into its centre. He commissioned many pioneering forms, such as the double-walled 'Blue' bowl by Henning Koppel, and the opaline glass-and-wood range designed by Jacob Bang in 1960.

The 1950s was a golden decade for Finnish glass, with Tapio Wirkkala and Timo Sarpaneva winning a range of international awards for their designs. Both men were based

ABOVE LEFT *Scandinavian glass can be richly coloured, etched with figures, overlaid with many textures or given a sandblasted finish. Simple pieces like the three vases shown here are effective in their emphasis on pure form over decorative style.*

ABOVE *Sleek glassware like this combines beauty and practicality in everyday objects. Scandinavian stemware is usually hand-blown, while stackable tumblers and highball glasses are generally part of pressed glassware ranges.*

at Iittala glassworks, where they created some of the firm's most supremely elegant and sophisticated designs. Wirkkala's work often found inspiration in nature's most dramatic forms, such as his arresting '*Jäävuori*', or 'Iceberg', vase of 1951 and his 'Solaris' centrifugally cast platter of 1974. At Iittala, Wirkkala produced an extensive body of work based on jagged ice blocks, lichen vessels and exotic mushroom shapes.

Sarpaneva's work seemed to move from functional objects to pure art and back again. His '*Lansetti*', or 'Lancet', pieces of the 1950s centred around the sculptural expression he found in creating a void-like air pocket within a solid crystal mass, while his 'i-collection' of modern household glasses for Iittala was driven by the challenge of bringing a sculptural approach to a utility range. In the 1960s, Iittala produced his 'Finlandia' range of 'frosted' vases, which acquired a richly textured finish from their moulds of alder wood as they became charred by the molten glass. The process ensured that each individual piece was unique, as the texture within the mould changed shape every time the mould was used.

Parallel to his role at the Finnish pottery factory Arabia, Kaj Franck created glass designs for the Finnish glassworks Nuutajärvi from the 1950s on. Franck's approach to glass was not dissimilar to his approach to ceramics – his glass tumblers and pitchers had the same clean lines as his '*Kilta*' ceramic service. While at Nuutajärvi, Franck made contributions to the glassware industry at large, by developing the means to standardize glass shapes and sizes, making them stackable and easier to store.

Less well known but no less significant for his contributions, the Finnish designer Göran Hongell was active in the 1950s, designing streamlined, undecorated glasses. In 1950, he designed the 'Aarne' glassware range produced today by Iittala, with smooth cylindrical bases that represent a tactile compromise between tumblers and wine glasses. Through the 'Aarne' range, Hongell revealed the importance of designing glasses that are just as pleasing to the touch as they are to the eye.

Today's glass designers are pioneering a fresh concept of what glass can be. Ingegerd Råman, Sweden's *grande dame* of glass, angles and curves simple lines along the streamlined shapes of her pieces. As she polishes or sandblasts her spare motifs into the surfaces of her 'Slow Fox' designs, she finds fresh expressions for everyday forms. Olle Brozén gives traditional glass objects a contemporary spirit by applying witty and irreverent motifs – cartoon cars, dreamy cityscapes and fashion silhouettes trace the curves of his designs.

Per B Sundberg, the *enfant terrible* of Scandinavian glass, takes an iconoclastic approach towards glass to express concepts more typically addressed by his artist contemporaries. Sundberg has taken the classical Graal method a step further in his '*Fabula*' technique, which enables him to use drawings and motifs without the distortion typically found in Graal. In one series, he renders a daring comic strip of La Ciccolina and Jeff Koons under the glass, while in others he creates surrealistic expressions of the natural world.

During the 1990s, Lena Bergström injected dynamism into Scandinavian glass, at a time when the industry had been criticized for being stagnant for two decades. Her designs contrasted sharply with the more subdued, classically elegant craftsmanship of the traditional Orrefors style. While her idiom is sculptural, with forms that often stem from the organic, her designs also assume geometric shapes that outline a vision for futuristic forms.

RIGHT *Whether angular or wavy, cubic or cylindrical, delicate or dense, the varied ranges of Scandinavian glass come together in a 'family' of unique styles. Lena Bergström's 'Puck' votive for Orrefors flickers beneath the top tier of this display unit, highlighting the contours of Alvar Aalto's iconic 'Savoy' vase and the silvery sheen of these metalwork vessels.*

Metalware

The vigorous, self-assured style of twentieth-century Scandinavian metalware encapsulates principles of traditional metal craftsmanship, jewellery design and fine art practice. Metal is beautifully sculpted into sleek contours, animal heads or geometric shapes and crafted with inlays of wood, glass, stone and jewels that are delightful to handle and to use.

The ancient craft of metalwork met modern design in the 1920s, when the Swedish silversmith Wiwen Nilsson embarked on his career as a designer at his family's silver workshop in Lund. His work, like that of his forebears, emphasized the unique lustre of the metal, which he crafted into sleek vessels and avant-garde jewellery that bore a distinctive modernist signature. Nilsson drew upon the classic techniques of his craft to create simplified forms with exquisite metalwork detailing that remain unrivalled in other decorative traditions. Although the fragile arts of ceramics and glass-blowing yield works of unparalleled expression, the durability of metalwork provides lasting designs that survive most other media. Nilsson approached metalware with the same considerations as an architect aiming to build a timeless edifice, aware that his enduring designs were destined to become iconic artefacts of the future.

Nilsson designed functional silver vessels with minimalistic shapes, unadorned surfaces and sleek geometric planes. In 1941, at the height of his career, he made a silver and ebony pitcher that proved to be one of his seminal works. He folded the silver into faceted ridges that contoured outwards around the pitcher's belly before tapering upwards to form the neck and spout. Its ebony handle was a perfect half-circle set level with the pitcher's rim, arcing downwards to meet the belly within a silver clasp.

In Stockholm, Estrid Ericson established the Svenskt Tenn company in 1924 to produce outstanding metalware exclusively in pewter. Her own designs were influenced by Chinese statues from the Ming period and Egyptian artefacts from Tutankhamen's tomb. Ericson set many of her early designs with semi-precious stones as if they were jewellery, later incorporating contemporary materials like Perspex (Plexiglas) or combining pewter with other metals to achieve a unique decorative effect. Ericson commissioned metalware from the leading Swedish designers of her day, such as Edvin Öhrström and Gunnar Cyrén, whose designs were so popular that they were said to sell out as fast as they could be cast at the foundry – even before they had time to cool down. Many of their classic works, along with pieces designed by Ericson herself and her colleague Josef Frank, are still in production today.

The Danish designer Henning Koppel produced a range of metalware pieces for Svenskt Tenn during the 1940s, then designed gold and silver jewellery for the Georg Jensen silver workshop when he returned to Denmark after the war. Koppel treated jewellery as wearable sculpture, designing stylized organic shapes in silver that linked to form necklaces and bracelets. He derived inspiration from the abstract works of art by the Romanian sculptor Constantin Brancusi and the French painter and sculptor Hans Arp, which he reflected in the sensuous, sculptural 'Caravel' silver cutlery set he designed for Georg Jensen in 1957. Koppel's pitchers, platters, serving dishes and bowls took on expressive, sweeping shapes that appeared to trap light within their cavities and harness reflections along their contours.

LEFT *The Danish silver workshop Georg Jensen is world-renowned for its supremely elegant metalware designs. Over the years, its elaborate neoclassical and art nouveau styles gave way to modern, minimalistic designs, like the nest of stainless steel bowls shown here.*

ABOVE *This stylized rendering of Poseidon by Wilhelm Kåge exemplifies the highly skilled craftsmanship of Nordic silversmiths and their affinity with classical themes.*

Piet Hein, the Danish mathematician, philosopher and designer, eschewed the abstract approach taken by Koppel and set about rationalizing the process of design. Hein endlessly explored the relationship between art and science to search for paradigms of enduring form and highbrow aesthetics. In his stainless steel candelabra '*Karlsvognen*', or 'The Great Bear', he set seven candleholders atop contoured stems of varying lengths that revolved like a stellar constellation, to mimic the constellation known as the Great Bear or Ursa Major.

While Arne Jacobsen is best known for his furniture designs and his architecture, the scope of his vision encompassed many metalware pieces. He devised his 'Cylinda Line' of cylindrical stainless steel for the Danish company Stelton in 1967, including an ice bucket, beakers and saucepans, all crafted with the monumental precision of architecture. He designed a teapot and a coffeepot as an exercise in ergonomics, placing the base of the spout near the bottom of each vessel's body and stretching its neck upwards above the level of the lid to minimize the possibility of spillage. Black handles were bolted to the vessel's sides, projecting outwards in a dramatic, angular silhouette offset by a circular space at the handle's centre. The overall effect was that of spatial geometry, created by juxtaposing streamlined cylindrical shapes with rectilinear handles.

Norway became known for its metalware at the end of the nineteenth century, after Gustav Gaudernack emigrated to Oslo from his native Bohemia in 1891. Gaudernack was one of the main exponents of the Nordic art nouveau style, designing metal bowls, vases, platters and glasses with exquisite decorative enamelling. His enamelling technique was revived in the 1950s by Grete Prytz, later known as Grete Korsmo through her marriage to the architect Arne Korsmo, and as Grete Prytz Kittelsen after Korsmo's death in 1968. Her distinctively abstract

BELOW FAR LEFT *Piet Hein was a mathematician as well as a designer. He studied an astronomical map of the Ursa Major constellation in order to calculate the dimensions of the 'Great Bear' candelabra shown below.*
BELOW LEFT *Traditional vernacular shapes continue to be hand-made in blacksmiths' forges today.*
BELOW *Estrid Ericson commissioned Karl Wojtech to design this coffee pot, creamer and sugar bowl for Svenskt Tenn in 1930.*

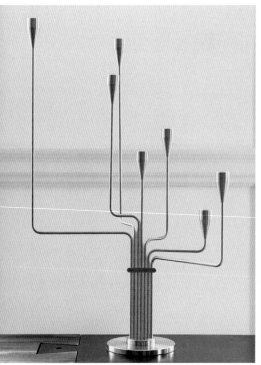

jewellery and metalware were enamelled in primary colours and produced by her family's firm, the Oslo silversmiths Jacob Tostrup. Her 'Domino' rings of 1952 were delicately enamelled but had a robust, masculine feel. In the 1970s Prytz designed enamelled stainless steel bowls and candelabra with colourful enamelled discs supporting each candle.

The Finnish metalware designer Bertel Gardberg established his studio in Helsinki in 1949 and subsequently designed and produced numerous pieces of award-winning metalware. His silver and teak tea range of the 1950s introduced a new aesthetic based on cubic forms and rippling, ring-shaped cooking pans. His silver tea caddy and chocolate pot replaced hard edges with rounded folds, and flattened bulbous shapes into sleek planes. 'Carelia', his stainless steel cutlery range of 1957, was produced in Finland but sold to an international market. In the 1970s, Gardberg received recognition for his jewellery, which he crafted in silver and set with precious and semi-precious stones. Like his metalware, each piece demonstrated a combination of modern innovation and timeless elegance.

ABOVE *Although Svenskt Tenn is probably best known for its furniture and textiles today, Estrid Ericson originally established the company to produce fine objects in pewter. Here, one of the two faces of the Roman god Janus sits among crystal decanters, while a cockerel and a heron perch on the shelf below. In the left-hand cupboard, the fine tableware and serving vessels from Svenskt Tenn are as functional as they are beautiful.*

Textiles

In Scandinavia today, the term 'textile' no longer has a simple definition. Whether described as wall hangings, soft furnishings, interior fabrics or artworks, Scandinavian textiles have an essential style that continues to bear traces of the homespun techniques passed down through generations of weavers. The traditional motifs that were circulated and exchanged among regions for centuries continue to find expression today in their original styles, or can be traced through pictorial references and figurative works that bear their influences. Nature was always reflected on the loom as it was in the other decorative arts. Many of today's abstract patterns are drawn in strong lines that convey a sense of interrelated spaces or suggest the border of land and sea or the meeting of mountains and sky.

'Textile art' is a term that has gained currency in Scandinavia in recent decades, describing both the tactile hanging fabrics that are made for domestic interiors and gallery spaces, as well as the bold illustrations or painterly motifs expressive enough to warrant mounting in a picture frame. It is not unusual to find framed textiles in a Scandinavian home – Josef Frank's '*Gröna Fåglar*', or 'Green Birds', is hung like a painting above the mantelpiece on page 132, and the Marimekko print on page 174 has also been mounted on a wooden frame like a canvas. Hand-printed textiles almost always take centre stage in the Scandinavian home, whether they are sewn into draperies and soft furnishings or acknowledged as the works of art that many of them genuinely are.

BELOW *Josef Frank followed the English tradition of using printed cretonne fabric for bedcovers, curtains, blinds and upholstery. The 'Aralia' fabric pictured here was designed by Frank in 1947 and has been in production ever since.*
RIGHT *Birgitta Hahn's 'Stads Biblioteket', or 'City Library', fabric is based on Erik Gunnar Asplund's design for the Stockholm City Library, built in 1928.*

Soft furnishings form the core of contemporary interior textiles in Scandinavia, where home fabrics have always been too beautiful to be stowed away until needed. While cushions, rugs, throws and curtains are often the most design-conscious of all interior textiles, they have never been aloof from the craft tradition. Nordic designers work in the same vocabulary as their craftsmen, remaining true to the integrity of the materials and the skill of the weavers. Although the textiles are practical enough to be indispensable and durable enough to last for decades, their elegant designs and soft textures make them as tactile as they are beautiful.

Urban themes and rural sensibilities merge together in the modern home, where textiles must strike a balance between functionality and pleasing display. The resurgence of fabrics from the 1930s, '40s and '50s proves the timelessness of Scandinavian designs, but also demonstrates the high quality of the original textiles, which remain in perfect condition after more than half a century of use. Despite advances in technology, these are reproduced today by the same processes that were used to print them all those years ago, revealing an unbroken tactile alliance between the freehand drawings of the designer, the soft touch of the printer's block and the satisfying feel of the finished material.

The spirit of contemporary Scandinavian textiles is rooted in simplicity, yet manages to incorporate many complex aspects of a single art form. Technical finesse, modern fibres and a range of fresh inspirations are used by today's textile designers as they dress the interior in visionary new fabrics, but the legacy of earlier styles and traditions remains ever-present.

Wall hangings

In the Nordic countries, textile design has been acknowledged as a fine art for many centuries. In a region where refined fibres were often scarce, hanging fabrics took on a significance beyond that of luxury and decoration. Early wall hangings depicted religious and ethical teachings, with pagan legends giving way to Christian doctrines in the Romanesque period. Many tapestries, nevertheless, were made for purely decorative purposes, celebrating the beauty of the natural world in scenes from the landscape, or woven with intricate decorative motifs. Over the years, their designs became richer and more stylized as they were embellished with embroidery and other needlework techniques.

Ever since the Norwegian Gerhard Munthe, who received acclaim as a painter before designing textiles, began practising in Norway in the 1880s, Scandinavian wall hangings have been celebrated throughout the world. Munthe acknowledged that the long lifespan of decorative textiles meant that they often survived their owners by several centuries, improving with age and becoming collectable items. He drew upon the past to design the icons of the future, finding inspiration in folklore, fables, legends and myths, as well as the flora of the Nordic landscape. The aesthetic that Munthe developed was considered to be the essence of all things Norwegian, articulated in a neo-Romantic style that echoed Norway's evolving expressions of national identity.

Munthe mined the Viking past for styles and motifs that would strengthen national spirit. Because so few original textiles from the Viking era had survived, he borrowed symbols from ancient woodcarving and metalwork in a brilliant synthesis of past and present. His use of vibrant greens, amber browns and ocean blues recalled the forest landscape, while sombre tones of grey and charcoal captured the colour of the mineral kingdom. The culmination of Munthe's oeuvre was his allegorical tapestry of 1903, which he gave the Danish name '*Den Kloge Fugl*', or 'The Wise Bird'. Drawing upon a Nordic fable as a source of inspiration, Munthe crafted a textural tableau of the ancient ruler who abandoned his palace to discover a wise bird taking refuge in a forest glade.

The Norwegian designer Frida Hansen was also an exponent of nationalistic revival styles, typically finding more inspiration in the vernacular weavings of the Norwegian countryside than in neo-Viking motifs. Her first tapestry was woven on a standing loom in the embroidery workshop she established in Stavanger in 1889. Her early inspirations were the textural equivalent of the Swedish *kurbits* style (see page 42), featuring biblical scenes traced by acanthus leaves or surrounded by trailing foliage. But after a trip to Paris, she abandoned the use of ancient motifs, devoting herself to the art nouveau style and becoming one of its greatest exponents in the textile arts. Despite their distinct stylistic differences, Hansen and Munthe often collaborated on tapestry designs, which Hansen produced under the auspices of *Det Norske Billedvæveri*, the weaving studio she established in Oslo in 1899.

In Copenhagen, Lis Ahlmann, like Munthe and Hansen, had studied painting before going on to become one of Denmark's greatest textile artists. Ahlmann accepted an apprenticeship as a weaver and soon became distinguished for the hanging textile panels she made. While she remained faithful to traditional craft techniques, such as weaving on a hand loom, for much of her life, she also designed textiles woven on power looms during the 1950s and '60s. Her simple checked patterns, parallel stripes and organic abstractions took shape in a muted palette of olive drab, coppery brown, yellow ochre and faded white. These textiles featured in the Design in Scandinavia exhibition that toured North America in the 1950s, and which generated interest in Ahlmann's approach. The popularity of her work made Ahlmann one of the key designers responsible for the post-war renaissance in Scandinavian textiles, and her work sparked the craze for minimalistic textiles that accompanied the Danish Modern movement.

Vibeke Klint, also a Danish textile artist, is considered by many to be Lis Ahlmann's spiritual heir. Ahlmann herself praised Klint's work, which transcended traditional styles to initiate a new generation of Danish textile design. Klint's wall hangings feature dramatic contrasting colour fields, in intense reds, bold yellows, deep blues and ivory whites. The hangings' simplicity has an extraordinary attraction, harnessing the power of colour to engage the eye. Klint's carpets, with their bold zigzags and geometric textures, are no less potent in their appeal. Her carpet collection of the 1950s is too beautiful to line the floor; as collectors' items today, the carpets are hung prominently at eye level.

The Finnish designer Dora Jung established her own textile studio in Helsinki in 1932, becoming well known for her tapestries. Jung beat the weft to create reliefs that gave her patterns a three-dimensional effect resembling Finland's traditional *rvijy* ('rug') wall hangings. Like many of the Danish and Swedish textile artists of her generation, Jung also turned to home textiles for innovation and experimentation. Her woven damask fabrics updated dining etiquette with modern table linen designs. Rather than imbuing them with floral patterns or simple flower repeats, Jung flattened the perspective of her woven flowers, turning them into abstract shapes. She also coloured them in a range of tints more akin to the autumn landscape than the blossoms of springtime. The abstract shapes and geometric patterns made the perfect backdrop for the utilitarian ceramics and tableware adorning the contemporary table.

ABOVE FAR LEFT *In an era when all artists strove to express the quintessentially Swedish, Maja Sjöström celebrated the national pastime of gathering wild berries in her 1903 'Red Berries' textile.*
ABOVE CENTRE LEFT *Märta Måås-Fjetterström is recognized as one of Sweden's foremost textile artists. Her work from the 1920s is characterized by rich, rhythmic patterns combined with Oriental references.*
ABOVE LEFT *During the inter-war years, Måås-Fjetterström also played a role in reviving the narrative tapestry tradition of the Middle Ages. The detail shown is a horse with a golden mane and tail, from her 'Unicorn in the Forest' wall hanging.*

Josef Frank

Josef Frank's textile designs span his entire career as a furniture designer and architect. Even before he moved to Sweden to work alongside Estrid Ericson at Svenskt Tenn, Frank had produced an extensive range of designs for printed fabrics and furnishings. Featuring geometrical figures or rich compositions of contrasting colours, Frank's tufted carpets resembled paved terraces or mosaic surfaces. Most of his work mined the natural kingdom for both the exotic and the everyday, which he portrayed in wavering, organic lines and abstract shapes that transcended the forms traditionally associated with flora and fauna.

Since childhood, Frank had displayed a strong interest in botany, and he drew flowers in a naturalistic manner that grew to characterize his work throughout his life. Many of his motifs were variations of flower forms, which he drew in flowing configurations and surreal colour schemes, intertwined among succulent berries, grapes, peaches, cherries and the leaves of trailing vines. Frank set pomegranates and citrus fruits amid an undergrowth of lush foliage or playfully depicted them in a style that mocked botanical illustrations. His flowers often seemed to hover between dream and reality, taking the shape of cloud-like swirls or the outlines of stars, with sharp-pointed petals and heart-shaped leaves.

Frank was fascinated by the exotic vegetation flourishing beyond the borders of Europe, exploring it throughout his career. His butterflies and cherry blossom recalled the exotic styles of the Far East, while his Chinese landscape designs reinterpreted the limpid forms of seventeenth-century Chinese paintings. From the landscape of Sri Lanka, Frank harvested the amoeba-shaped leaves, tiger-striped flowers and speckled vine fruits depicted in his

LEFT *Josef Frank's 'Brazil' motif was based on the succulent flowers and colourful fruits of the equatorial landscape. The pattern dates back to 1943 and was designed for printing on heavy Swedish linen. Here, 'Brazil' fabric has been made into lavish curtains, creating a wall of exotic flora and spectacular colours.*

RIGHT *The hand-knotted 'Carpet No. 1', which was designed in 1938, is considered one of Josef Frank's most accomplished works. The carpet's grey background resembles a paved terrace, while many of the design idioms are loosely based on geometrical figures. The lateral strokes of colour near the border and the crimson five-pointed star were, however, inspired by motifs found in Tutankhamen's tomb. Although keen to feature abstractions of flowers and birds in his carpet designs, Frank also believed, sentimentally, that their images should not be stepped on.*

'Ceylon' design. In 'Tehran', he drew a cornucopia of looping vines, tri-forked foliage, red tree branches and sprays of delicate white blossoms growing against the velvety darkness of a night sky. His foray into the Himalayas led to a textile named after them, in which he downscaled the precipitous peaks into volcano craters and conical mounds overgrown with orchids, calla lilies, bluebells, daisies and succulent fruits.

Frank explored the Caribbean islands in order to research a floral network of indigo colours, fluted petals and palmate leaves, and he then ducked below the equator to find a vibrant fusion of textured fruits, blossoming flowers and slender creepers in Brazil. Progressing to Argentina to draw upon the lush vegetation of the vast river estuary that lies outside Buenos Aires, he twinned and interlaced vines and plant stems to form a breezy tropical network in cool tones of blue and white.

Closer to home, Frank drew inspiration from the Swedish summer garden, the Nordic flora of forest glades, and the alpine meadows of his native Austria. He brought the summer flora of the Austrian mountains to the Scandinavian winter in his 'Ögontröst', or 'Eyebright', motif, which was printed on linen. Originally named 'Kitzbühel', *Ögontröst* was one of around twenty Viennese textile designs that he took with him when he settled in Sweden. '*Bolero*', '*Frühling*', '*Dryade*' and '*Samara*' were printed by the Viennese *Haus & Garten* magazine in the 1920s and early '30s. Svenskt Tenn reprinted Frank's '*Orangenweige*' in the 1930s, followed by '*Hügel*', which was renamed '*Kullarna*', or 'The Hills', and printed in the 1940s.

Frank revisited the classical Indian tree of life design depicted on so many chintzes throughout the centuries. The tree of life symbolizes the life force and the continued renewal of life through successive generations of living creatures. Frank's '*Gröna Fåglar*', or 'Green Birds', print on linen depicts a flock of green birds on a flowering tree, perching on its branches and near its mangrove roots. Starlings, doves and parrots chirp and sing, while ducks and herons paddle in the blue stream flowing beneath them. Frank slanted the tree towards the left, but maintained equilibrium through the birds' horizontal position.

Today, the textile motifs that Frank designed over three decades continue to form the core of Svenskt Tenn's textile line. Of the 125 fabric patterns printed during Frank's lifetime, about forty of them live on as textile classics. Their bold designs and artistic styles have a timeless spirit that remains strong long after their colours have begun to fade.

Jobs Handtryck

The intricate designs and delicate motifs drawn by the Jobs family have been hand-printed for several generations, ever since Peer Jobs began experimenting with textile printing in the 1930s. After he had established his workshop – Jobs Handtryck ('Hand Printing') – in Västanvik, a tiny village in the beautiful Swedish province of Dalarna, his sisters Gocken and Lisbet joined him, and they went on to produce some of the most gorgeous textiles ever made in Sweden.

The Jobs sisters conjured a world of colourful enchantment. Their dreamy flower motifs had a vibrancy and elan that captured the spirit of the local landscape, which was the physical and spiritual centre of Sweden's craft traditions. The craftsmen of Dalarna were known for their almost pagan reverence for the natural world, which they translated into decorative forms, such as *kurbits* painting (see page 42). Gocken decorated textiles with painterly representations of the wildflowers that grew in the surrounding countryside, which she evoked with an enchanting sensitivity. Dandelions, buttercups, wild arum lilies, ferns, wild roses and sunflowers were drawn in lush motifs, where butterflies, bees and dragonflies perched on the delicate petals or flew undisturbed among the succulent foliage.

Gocken Jobs imbued her work with a poetic lyricism that turned each of her figurative textiles into a fairy tale. In 1945 she designed her 'Gobelin' nursery hanging – playfully named after the French Gobelins tapestry workshop – featuring many elements that, together, paint a vivid picture of pastoral Swedish life. Gustavian interiors, baroque manor houses and medieval fortresses were shown alongside the copper vessels, *Dalahästar* (painted wooden horses), rag rugs, straw ornaments

BELOW *Dagmar Lodén's 'Tistlar', or 'Thistle', motifs, designed in 1949, are among Jobs Handtryck's most spectacular fabrics. The motifs have the sophisticated expression of an artist's palette, while their vibrant red or electric blue backgrounds make them ideal choices for the nursery.*

and carved chests that characterized the craft tradition. Gocken drew dancing girls and serenading troubadours who moved amid flying birds, dancing dogs and paddling ducks, sidestepping the dutiful figures occupied with spinning, weaving or dressmaking.

Peer Jobs's wife, Eva, devoted more than forty years to textile design, creating over thirty acclaimed motifs during her career. Working in collaboration with the Nordic Museum in Stockholm, she reproduced many designs from the nineteenth century in the summertime printing workshop she opened there at Skansen. Eva commissioned textiles from several new designers, whose work became as popular as her own. Cecilia Hall, for example, designed the colourful 'Morfars Trädgård', or 'Grandmother's Orchard', and 'Paradisträd', or 'Paradise Tree', both of which became immediate successes. Ingela Backman's magnificent 'Löjtnantshjärta', or 'Bleeding Heart', captured the essence of springtime and the crisp beauty of wildflowers.

Many of Gocken's and Lisbet's designs continue to be revered today, and several are still in production. They also commissioned textiles from designers such as Carl Malmsten, Dagmar Lodén, Sune Sundahl, Erik Andersson and Kjell Löwenadler, whose works are acknowledged as design classics today. Lodén's dynamic 'Tistlar', or 'Thistles', textile of 1949 was one of the most exciting textiles Jobs Handtryck ever produced. The thistles are depicted with menacing, jagged barbs and thorny stems. Each element of plant life seems to take on a predatory role, keeping the observer at a distance rather than drawing them closer. While nature was traditionally sweetened and made more romantic in Swedish textile motifs, Lodén's design was a witty reversal that presented an alternative view of the natural world.

Marimekko

The Finnish textile company Marimekko emerged in the austere milieu of the post-war years, when fabric was rationed and colourful pigments were difficult to obtain. Wartime grey, oilcloth and artificial silk were virtually the only interior fabrics available, and home textiles had been darned and patched for nearly a decade owing to the shortage of cloth.

In Helsinki, the small textile-printing workshop owned by Viljo Ratia eventually secured an official permit to manufacture oilcloth. The firm would have started producing the floral patterns that dominated Finland at that time, had Armi Ratia, Viljo's wife and an arts graduate, not intervened. Baulking at her husband's request to devise a floral repeat, she designed instead the 'Kaisla', or 'Reed', pattern of repeating reeds, which was drawn in bold silhouettes and strong colours. 'Kaisla' was an instant success, and this encouraged Ratia to continue designing other patterns in her spare time. Her designs were non-figurative, daring experiments in colour, and were innovative in their neutrality. The textiles were neither flowery and feminine nor starkly masculine, neither routinely conventional nor breathtakingly radical.

ABOVE *Erik Andersson's 'Kronprinsen', or 'Crown Prince', design marks a historic royal visit to Sweden's Dalarna region. The textile depicts the 1831 journey of the future King Oscar I, who acceded to the Swedish throne in 1844. The crown prince is surrounded by the folkloric* kurbits *motifs that typify the style of this region.*

Orders flooded in and Ratia found herself too busy to continue designing. Maija Isola, a young painter, came on board as the company's first design director. Isola's task was to interpret Ratia's design ethos visually, and express her aesthetic vision in a range of interior fabrics. These were the first textiles sold under the Marimekko label. Although it translates into English as 'Mari's little skirt', the name 'Marimekko' was chosen not for its fashion connotations but for its ease of pronunciation in the other Nordic tongues and in languages around the globe. Because the name is spelled with letters of the alphabet also found on a non-Scandinavian typewriter, it could be correctly written in any typeface.

Ratia regarded her first soft furnishings as 'stage props for the living environment', because she initially manufactured them only to show her audience how the textiles could be used. Streamlined functionality and playful practicality were incorporated into the Marimekko manifesto. Ratia described the range as a common ground for two very opposite characters from *Seven Brothers*, Aleksis Kivi's classic Finnish tale of 1870 – the practical Venla and the ethereal Anna. In Scandinavia and abroad, Marimekko quickly appealed to the fashion-conscious, design-led upper-middle and upper classes – more to the lofty aspirations of Anna than the earthiness of Venla.

At the height of Marimekko's success, Anna and Venla, not to mention the seven brothers, their Scandinavian siblings and their international cousins, all seemed united by the Marimekko label. The American distribution was managed by an architect's office, which marketed the textiles as a means of creating a room rather than merely decorating it, by generating a more dynamic sense of visual space. From the mid-1950s, American sofas, curtains and armchairs were covered in Marimekko materials, and so were Americans themselves. When, in 1958, Jackie Kennedy was criticized by the press for her exclusive Paris fashions, she immediately purchased seven Marimekko items, which radically changed her image.

Ratia's concept of the woman who bought her interior textiles was the 'Mari Girl', an independent woman who took pleasure in entertaining at home as much as she enjoyed going out – and, ideally, would be married to an architect. The Mari Girl lived in a 'flexibly changing space', according to the Swedish newspaper *Dagens Nyeter* in 1967, which went on to explain how the Mari Girl attained this: 'This is cheapest and easiest to achieve with textiles; curtains, tablecloths, hangings and counterpanes, which are easy to change around, thus creating different colour schemes and atmospheres. She has a pile of Maija Isola's textiles ready-hemmed in the cupboard and with them, she continually furnishes her home.'

The autumn and winter collections of Maija Isola's iconic fabric prints are even more popular today than when they were first manufactured in the 1950s and '60s. Some classic designs are now produced in a wider range of colours, notably the famous yellow poppies of the '*Unikko*' fabric, which now bloom against crimson, blue, or green backgrounds.

The secret of Marimekko's continued success seems to be its expression of the Nordic attitude to life, and the flexible textile 'props' designed to sustain it in the home environment. Today, the company continues to be associated with fashion and other elements of Finnish design such as furniture, glassware and dining. Marimekko never ceases to offer something new and original, even if it simply revisits its own classical designs to create contemporary icons of the textile world.

LEFT *Marimekko is best known for its fashion designs, but the label began as a means of expanding its range of interior textiles. The sharp silhouette of the 'Ruusupuu' textile, designed by Maija Isola in 1957, takes on the graphic appearance of an artwork as it is mounted on a wall. 'Ruusupuu' is atypical of Isola's designs and is often mistaken for the work of Ulla Ericson-Åström.*

ABOVE *Maija Isola's vibrant 'Unikko' print from1960 became one of Marimekko's most popular interior motifs. Isola printed her boldly abstracted designs on durable cotton cloth suitable for both fashions and soft furnishings.*

ABOVE *Swedish textile designers are reviving the Afghan coats of the 1970s – but as blankets, rugs and wall hangings. The curly fleece of Anatolian mountain goats is dyed in blazing colours and hand-sewn into the textiles' weave. Pia Wallén's 'Cross' rug relies on its graphic outline rather than texture to create an eye-catching effect.*

Contemporary designers

While Scandinavian textiles have earned a reputation for innovation and individuality today, for many years textile artists were restricted to designing muted patterns and pastoral motifs that would appeal to the mass market. This changed radically in the late 1960s, as a revolutionary spirit swept through Sweden, and the textile cooperative *10-gruppen* – 'The Group of Ten' – was born. It was formed by ten Swedish textile designers, all of whom shared a common design idiom of brightly coloured designs with bold, pop art-like motifs. Banding together to form an independent manufacturing company enabled the designers themselves to dictate the quality of the designs and the length of their production runs. By taking control of the manufacturing process, they were able to make decisions in the interest of artistic integrity rather than being obliged to shape their designs according to market demands.

The group commissioned Borås Wäfveri, an independent Swedish textile manufacturer, to produce their first collection of ten designs in 1972. A year later, *10-gruppen* opened its own fabric shop in Stockholm, successfully marketing its non-conformist interior textiles internationally. The 'Joy' collection of 1980 was particularly popular in France, where the fabrics were bought by fashion houses as well as interior designers.

Over the years, the group produced ready-made ranges of bedlinen, table linen, curtains and upholstery fabrics in both playful patterns and high-design motifs. Gunilla Axén's 1972 design '*Hundar*', or 'Dogs', which resembles a comic strip of pet dogs barking in air bubbles, became a classic favourite of children and adults alike. Her '*Moln*' fabric, with its static clouds and sky-blue background, is equally timeless in its appeal. The wavering lines and bold stripes of Tom Hedqvist's designs became the graphic motifs that were used on Swedish milk cartons, extending his style vocabulary beyond the surface of fabrics. Today, only three of the original ten founders – Ingela Håkansson, Birgitta Hahn and Tom Hedqvist – remain active in *10-gruppen*, but it continues to produce a popular range of interior textiles through a long-standing collaboration with Borås Wäfveri.

Against this background, the Swedish textile designer Pia Wallén has become a designer of international repute. Wallén has devoted two decades to studying the sculptural and textural characteristics of a variety of traditional textiles. One of the most influential textile designers working in Scandinavia today, she transformed felt from a neglected material into the chic household textile of the 1990s. Her felt slippers have virtually become a design classic, their cosy fit and contrasting zigzag stitching demonstrating just how beautiful industrial felt can be. Wallén even designed a range of sleek silver jewellery fitted with supple

THIS PAGE *Pia Wallén's 'Cross' blankets and rugs feature a universal symbol that appeals to cultures all over the world. The 'Cross' blanket shown here was designed in contrasting black and white wools, but the range also includes vibrant primary colours.*

felt linings, blurring the boundaries between textiles and metalwork. 'Cross', the repeated equilateral cross-motif on blankets that Wallén created for Element Design, was for several years her signature design. The cross configuration appealed to Wallén as both a symbol and a motif, and had a strong resonance with design-savvy individuals around the world.

Wallén's 'Dot' collection of 2000 includes a range of soft furnishings in different-coloured felts, encompassing household bags and bowls along with woollen carpets. Her rectilinear 'Dot' carpets feature patterns of domino-like circles in bold relief, giving the surface of the carpets a distinctive three-dimensional feel and making their tactile properties appeal to the eye as well as to the hand.

Asplund, a Stockholm-based firm of textile, carpet and furniture manufacturers, breathed new life into the Scandinavian textile design scene when it was established in 1990. Asplund has commissioned carpets from a range of designers, including Pia Wallén from Sweden, Anki Gneib from Finland and Thomas Sandell (born in Finland and brought up in Sweden). The company forged an important link between art and textile design when it commissioned the Swedish art duo Bigert & Bergström to design a wool carpet. Coloured in deep crimson and completely devoid of ornamentation, 'Egg', as the carpet came to be called, is true to the oval outline that its name suggests.

Asplund commissions textiles from designers around the world, bringing a wealth of international talent to Scandinavian interior fabrics. The carpet 'Marc' designed by Marc Newson from Australia is completely covered with a serpentine motif that interconnects laterally, vertically and diagonally. A minimalistic monochrome carpet subtly decorated in a striped relief was designed by the Argentinian designer Alfredo Häberli. The vibrant red fibres of the carpet resonate with warmth and colour, making a powerful visual statement whether it lines the floor or adorns the wall.

The visionary textile firm Designer's Eye, creator of a range of award-winning fabrics, operates from studios in the Swedish province of Skåne. The Swedish designer Lena Bergström, also known for her award-winning glass designs, brought Designer's Eye to the forefront of Swedish design with her abstract wall hangings and stylized interior textiles. The work of Elsie Arenlind, also an award-winning Swedish designer, parallels the streamlined creations of Bergström. Their combined range of designs numbers among the most sought-after interior textiles in Scandinavia today.

Designer's Eye's spare vocabulary of classic shapes, natural earth tones, and primary reds and blues is used to create breathtakingly simple designs that take minimalism to a higher level. Despite the textiles' international appeal, the firm draws upon principles that are distinctively Scandinavian, to produce traditional woven textiles expressed in an ultra-contemporary way. While its *raison d'être* is to offer soft furnishings that are well designed and exquisitely produced, it manages to craft them into designs that can be reconfigured into new forms or even assume the functions of furniture, such as a screen.

Designer's Eye produces a varied range of cushion covers, quilted cushions, wall hangings, table runners and fabric throws. The textile designs generally remain true to the parallel lines and grid patterns of the weaving process, and most of their shapes are geometrical and linear. The outlines are so spare that to label them 'motifs' would be an

LEFT *The Stockholm company Asplund's rug collections breathed new life into the Scandinavian carpet industry with strikingly simple designs. Its carpets typically feature a graphic motif or rely on a textured surface to create a repeating pattern. From the late 1990s on, Asplund began to invite designers from outside Scandinavia to contribute to its repertoire. This detail is taken from the interlocking motif of Marc Newson's carpet for Asplund, simply titled 'Marc'.*

exaggeration. Broad bands of colour are divided into contrasting fields, or separated into individual strips of colour. The cushion covers are typically trimmed in overlock, or subtly traced with braid to give a relief effect along the surface of the textile.

Although Bergström and Arenlind eschew floral motifs, they are true to nature nonetheless. Their designs attest to the potency of natural colours and the irrefutable allure of organic fabrics. The textiles are woven in 100 per cent wool, which has been carefully chosen from sheep farms in continental Europe to supply seductively soft fabrics. Designer's Eye maintains that the importance of the interplay between the body and the fabric it rests on should never be underestimated.

Bergström's wall hangings are sized to stretch from the ceiling to the floorboards in a visual sweep of texture, colour and motif. Blocks of parallel lines form repeating patterns separated by wide bands of colour, balancing the linearity of the blocks. Her free-standing 'Wall' room divider, which is constructed from a series of wood and metal battens, is covered in woollen quilting to provide a playfully sculptural partition. 'Wall' can be unrolled and stood upright in a matter of seconds, constituting one of the most innovative screens and interesting textile designs in Sweden today.

The high-tech fabrics of Icelandic textile designer Margret Adolfsdóttir are popular among both fashion designers and interior designers. Through the use of lasers, Adolfsdóttir carves geometric patterns in wall hangings, screens, upholstery and a range of other soft furnishings. Using both synthetic materials and natural fibres, she often overlays a smooth textile with a laser-cut fabric to give a textured effect or a three-dimensional motif. Her unique application of print techniques, dye methods and laser cuttings seems set to create the soft furnishings of the future as she suffuses the interior with geometric motifs and abstract shapes.

The Oslo-based design studio Liminal is definitely going places. Shortly after it formed in Oslo in 2001, Liminal was sponsored by the Norwegian government to represent the country's burgeoning design culture at exhibitions in London and Milan. The partnership between the Finnish textile artist Sari Syväluoma and the Norwegian product designer Catherina Lande has yielded a dynamic range of soft furnishings, metalware, glass and ceramics. Designed to be draped over chairs, sofas, beds and windows as a form of textile art in the home, Syväluoma's fabrics constitute part of her vision to create a clutter-free interior. Her fabrics metamorphose into curtains, upholstery and cushions with precise and powerful designs that eclipse the need for paint finishes, elaborate carpets or decorative detailing in the room. Used on an antique chair, her ultra-contemporary upholstery breathes new life into old furniture. Syväluoma treats an entire room as an artist would a canvas, using a palette of soft colours and gentle textures to build up layers of fabric with the careful composition of a still life.

Whether expressed in subtle textile motifs or in understated, sculptural forms, the essential simplicity of Scandinavian design continues to be at the heart of the Nordic interior today as it has been for several centuries. As the subdued luxuries of Scandinavian design transform the classical hallmarks of the past into new inspiration for the present, they also outline a fresh direction for the styles of tomorrow.

OPPOSITE *As an extension of her 'Slit' glassware designs, Lena Bergström designed a range of hanging textiles with delicate perforations that allow light to pass through.*

THIS PAGE *The muted motifs of Sari Syväluoma's 'Juicy' fabric express freedom and exuberance as they travel across the textile.*

DIRECTORY OF DESIGNERS

A general guide to today's leading Scandinavian designers.

The Swedes

ALEXANDER LERVIK
Västerlånggatan 27
SE-11129 Stockholm
T + 46 8 22 22 01
mail@alexanderlervik.com

ANKI GNEIB
Riddargatan 28
SE-11457 Stockholm
T + 46 7 09 50 70 91
pohl.gneib@telia.com

ANNA VON SCHEWEN
Guldgränd 1
SE-11820 Stockholm
T + 46 8 643 6220
anna.vonschewen@telia.com

ANN WÅHLSTRÖM
Folkungagatan 114-116
SE-11630 Stockholm
T + 46 8 641 2002
ann.wahlstrom@chello.se

ÅKE AXELSSON
Birger Jarlsgatan 57
SE-11356 Stockholm
T + 46 8 442 9150
info@galleristolen.se

BJÖRN DAHLSTRÖM
Frejgatan 20
SE-11349 Stockholm
T + 46 8 673 4200
dahlstrom@dahlstromdesign.se

BLÅ STATION
Box 100
Sandvaktaregatan 17
SE-29622 Åhus
T + 46 4 424 9070
info@blastation.se

BOX DESIGN
Repslagargatan 17B
SE-11846 Stockholm
T + 46 8 640 1212
ann@boxdesign.se

CLAESSON KOIVISTO RUNE
Sankt Paulsgatan 25
SE-11848 Stockholm
T + 46 8 644 5863
arkitektkontor@claesson-koivisto-rune.se

ELSIE ARENLIND
Gässlingavägen 11
SE-29144 Kristianstad
T + 46 4 421 9230
elsie.arenlind@designerseye.se

FILIPPA NAESS
51 Kinnerton Street
London SW1X 8ED
T + 44 20 7235 1722
filippa@dircon.co.uk

INGEGERD RÅMAN
SE-38040 Orrefors
T + 46 4 813 4000
ingegerd.raman@orrefors.se

INGELA HEDLUND CLAXTON
6 Cromwell Grove
London W6 7RG
T + 44 20 7603 3799
ingelaclaxton@hotmail.com

JONAS BOHLIN
Södermalmstorg 4
SE-11645 Stockholm
T + 46 8 615 2389
info@jonasbohlindesign.com

JONAS LINDVALL
Tågmästargatan 2
SE-21130 Malmö
T + 46 4 030 2100
info@vertigo.m.se

LENA BERGSTRÖM
SE-38040 Orrefors
T + 46 4 813 4000
lena.bergstrom@orrefors.se

MATS THESELIUS
Adelbergsvägen 4
SE-27332 Tomelilla
T + 46 4 171 5208
mats@theselius.com

MATTIAS LJUNGGREN AB
Timmermansgatan 5,
SE-11825 Stockholm
T + 46 8 16 00 44

OLLE ANDERSON
White Design
Box 2502
Magasinsgatan 10
SE-40317 Gothenberg
T + 46 3 160 8771
olle.anderson@white.se

OREFELT ASSOCIATES
Unit 43, Pall Mall Deposit
124–128 Barlby Road
London W10 6BL
T + 44 20 8960 2560
mail@orefelt.demon.co.uk

PER B SUNDBERG
SE-38040 Orrefors
T + 46 4 813 4000
per.sundberg@orrefors.se

PIA TÖRNELL
Box 903
Fiskaregatan 4
SE-53119 Lidköping
T + 46 5 108 2300
rorstrand.info@designor.com

PIA WALLÉN
Narvavägen 7
SE-11460 Stockholm
T + 46 8 665 3329
info@piawallen.com

SALDO GROUP
Södra Kaserngatan 7
SE-29131 Kristianstad
T + 46 4 412 6181
mailbox@saldo.com

SHIDEH SHAYGAN
5 Sebastian Street
London EC1V 0HD
T + 44 77 98 73 39 77
shideh.shaygan@telia.com

THOMAS ERIKSSON
Riddargatan 17D
SE-11457 Stockholm
T + 46 8 55 55 18 00
info@teark.se

THOMAS SANDELL
Riddargatan 17D
SE-11457 Stockholm
T + 46 8 50 62 17 00
info@sandellsandberg.se

UGLYCUTE
St Paulsgatan 28A
SE-11848 Stockholm
T + 46 8 658 4440
info@uglycute.com

10-GRUPPEN
Götgatan 25
SE-11646 Stockholm
T + 46 8 643 2504
info@tiogruppen.com

The Danes

ANNE LISE KJAER
Kjaer Global
33 Hugo Road
London N19 5EU
T + 44 20 7607 6521
info@kjaer-global.com

ERIK BAGGER
Fortunvej 87
DK-2920 Charlottenlund
T + 45 3 963 8566
fob@erikbagger.dk

HANS SANDGREN-JAKOBSEN
Færgevej 3
DK-8500 Grenaa
T + 45 8 632 0048
mail@hans-sandgren-jakobsen.com

KARIN MICHELSEN
Keramisk Værksted
Wilders Plads 9B
DK-1403 Copenhagen
T + 45 3 296 2920
kamik@post7.tele.dk

LIN UTZON
Bøssemagergade 64
DK-3150 Hellebæk
T + 45 4 025 9928
lin@utzon.com

LOTTE THORSØE
Fjelstedvej 10
DK-9550 Mariager
T + 45 9 854 2921
lottethorsoe@mail.tele.dk

MATHIAS BENGTSSON
Studio 2
30 Aldridge Road Villas
London W11 1BW
T + 44 20 7792 8964
bengtssondesign@hotmail.com

NANNA DITZEL
Klareboderne 4
DK-1115 Copenhagen
T + 45 3 393 9480

**NIELS GAMMELGAARD
& LARS MATHIESEN**
Pelikan Design
Vestergade 10 / 4SAL
DK-1456 Copenhagen
T + 45 3 333 9950
niels@pelikan.dk

NIELS KJELDSEN
Webersgade 9 / 5
DK-2100 Copenhagen
T + 45 4 025 7580
nk@niels-kjeldsen.dk

SEBASTIAN HOLMBÄCK
Viborggade 47A
DK-2100 Copenhagen
T + 45 4 015 4571
sebastian.h@mobilixnet.dk

**TEGNESTUEN VANDKUNSTEN
ARCHITECTS**
Bådmandsstraede 6
DK-1407 Copenhagen
T + 45 3 254 2111
vandkunsten@vandkunst.dk

THEA BJERG
Herman Triers Plads 5
DK-1631 Copenhagen
T + 45 3 535 3166
theabjerg@hotmail.com

TINA RATZER
Ryesgade 19
DK-2200 Copenhagen
T + 45 3 535 0899
tina.ratzer@mobilixnet.dk

TOBIAS JACOBSEN
Ryesgade 19C
DK-2200 Copenhagen
T + 45 3 535 0592
mail@tobiasjacobsen.dk

TORBEN QUAADE
Wesselsgade 5/1
DK-2200 Copenhagen
T+ 45 3 646 1333
torben@quaade.net

VIBEKE ROHLAND
St Kongensgade 75B
DK-1264 Copenhagen
T + 45 3 391 0044
vibekerohlandesign@kabelnettet.dk

The Norwegians

ANNE MARI MEHUS
Karlstadgata 12
N-0553 Oslo
T + 47 4 522 8961
a_mehus@hotmail.com

ANNE THOMASSEN
Revefaret 6
N-0491 Oslo
T + 47 4 166 2671
athom6@hotmail.com

CATHERINA LANDE
Liminal
Larviksgata 3
N-0468 Oslo
T + 47 9 766 9239
catherina@liminal-design.com

CATHRINE MASKE
Eirik Raudes vei 21
N-0196 Oslo
T + 47 9 174 3146
cmaske@frisurf.no

DTANK
Pilestredet 75C
N-0354 Oslo
T + 47 22 60 19 44
www.dtank.no

FREDRIK TORSTEINSEN
Lommedalsveien 189A
N-1353 Bæruns Verk
T + 47 6 713 0030
post@torsteinsen.no

FRODE MYHR
Stemmeveien 8
N-5009 Bergen
T + 47 5 531 9029
funkyfrode@hotmail.com

JENS OLAV HETLAND
Vestre Håbakken 2
N-4340 Bryne
T + 47 5 148 2290
jensolav@hetland.as

JOHAN VERDE
Jonsrudveien 14
N-0265 Oslo
T + 47 9 139 3244
j-verde@online.no

K8
Waldemar Thranes gate 75
N-0175 Oslo
T + 47 2 211 4056
k8@k8.no

MARTIN OTTO FOUGNER
Mads Pedersens gate 7
N-2318 Hamar
T + 47 9 170 3190
martin.otto.fougner@broadpark.no

NORWAY SAYS
Thorvald Meyers gate 15
N-0555 Oslo
T + 47 2 238 2575
info@norwaysays.com

OHM DESIGN
Fagerborg gate 42
N-0169 Oslo
info@ohmdesign.no

PER IVAR LEDANG
Fredriksborg gade 46
DK-1360 Copenhagen
T + 45 3 393 3310
info@ledangdesign.dk

PIA MYRVOLD
65 Boulevard de Strasbourg
75010 Paris
T + 33 1 45 23 15 42
studio@pia-myrvold.com

RONNI STRØM
Westye Egebergs gate 3A
N-0177 Oslo
T + 47 9 223 9767
mail@upnorth.no

SNØHETTA
Christian Krohgs gate 32B
N-0186 Oslo
T + 47 2 298 8230
info@snoarc.no

TIAS ECKHOFF
Norsk Stålpress
PO Box 3440
Yrte Sandviken
N-5815 Bergen
info@norstaal.no

SOURCES

The Finns

AGNETA HOBIN
Ripusuontie 42A
FIN-00660 Helsinki
T + 358 9 724 2743

BJÖRN WECKSTRÖM
Kluuvikatu 2
FIN-00100 Helsinki
T + 358 9 65 65 29
leila.weckstrom@bjornweckstrom.com

HARRI KOSKINEN
Friends of Industry
Lemuntie 4D
FIN-00510 Helsinki
T + 358 9 72 68 90 90
harri@harrikoskinen.com

ILKKA SUPPANEN
Punavuorenkatu 1 / A7
FIN-00120 Helsinki
T + 358 9 62 27 87 37
info@suppanen.com

IMU / FINNISH NATIONAL DESIGN TEAM
Lemuntie 4D
FIN-00510 Helsinki
T + 358 5 05 77 98 89
imu@imudesign.org

KERTTU NURMINEN
Nuutajärvi Glass
FIN-31160 Nuutajärvi
T + 358 2 04 39 15
kerttu.nurminen@iittala.fi

SARI SYVÄLUOMA
Liminal
Larviksgata 3
N-0468 Oslo
T + 47 9 309 4515
sari@liminal-design.com

STEFAN LINDFORS
Albertinkatu 23A /21
FIN-00120 Helskinki
T + 358 4 05 56 01 64
hoppania@diiva.fi

TIMO SALLI
Meritullinkatu 11
FIN-00170 Helsinki
T + 358 9 68 13 77 00
salli@timosalli.com

TIMO SARPANEVA
Iittala Glass
FIN-14500 Iittala
T + 358 2 04 39 15
marjatta.sarpaneva@sarpaneva.com

TONFISK DESIGN
Kivipyykintie 6
FIN-00710 Helsinki
T + 358 9 72 31 60 60
info@tonfisk-design.fi

VALVOMO
Perämiehenkatu 12E
FIN-00150 Helsinki
T + 358 9 612 2310
info@valvomo.com

The Icelandics

DÖGG GUðMUNDSDÓTTIR
Daneskiold Samsøes A 40
DK-1434 Copenhagen
T + 45 3 585 3635
dogg@doggdesign.com

EINAR THORSTEINSSON
Proskauerstr 10
D-10247 Berlin
T + 49 30 42 80 94 32
cl-berlin@kingdomes.de

HLYNUR VAGN ATLASON
84 Forsyth Street #3R
New York, NY 10002
T + 1 646 418 3416
atlason@atlason.com

HRAFNKELL BIRGISSON
Choriner Strasse 31
D-10435 Berlin
T + 49 30 441 8889
design@hrafnkell.com

ICELAND DESIGN
Jülicher Straße 373
D-52070 Aachen
T + 49 2 41 41 35 34 10
dc@iceland-design.com

KATRIN PÉTURSDÓTTIR & MICHAEL YOUNG
PO Box 498
IS-101 Reykjavík
T + 354 561 2327
katrin.petursd@lhi.is
michaelyoung@simnet.is

MARGRET ADOLFSDÓTTIR
81 Sandown Road
Brighton BN2 3EH
T + 44 1273 609 089
sa-tex@dircon.co.uk

OLAFUR THORDARSON
Dingaling Studio, Inc.
44 Trinity Place
New York, NY 10006
T + 1 212 482 0208
olafur@dingaling.net

SIGURðUR GÚSTAFSSON
Klapparstígur 16
IS-101 Reykjavík
T + 354 552 2860
arksg@islandia.is

STUDIO GRANDA
Smidjustigur 11B
IS-101 Reykjavík
T + 354 562 2661
studiogranda@studiogranda.is

THORVALDUR THORSTEINSSON
14658 Killion St
Los Angeles, CA 91411
T + 1 818 904 5920
thorval@vortex.is

For local outlets, visit the websites listed below or telephone for details.

ARABIA
Hämeentie 135
FIN-00560 Helsinki
T + 358 204 3911
www.arabia.fi

ARTEK
Eteläesplanadi 18
FIN-00130 Helsinki
T + 358 9 61 61 32 50
www.artek.fi

ARTEK UK
13 New North Street
London WC1N 3PJ
T + 44 20 7420 5913
www.artek.fi

ASPLUND
Sibyllegatan 31
SE-11442 Stockholm
T + 46 8 662 5284
www.asplund.org

BO CONCEPT
Mørupvej 16
DK-7400 Herning
T + 45 7 013 1366
www.boconcept.com

BODA NOVA-HÖGANÄS KERAMIK
Box 23
SE-26321 Höganäs
T + 46 4 236 1154
www.bodanova.se

BORÅS WÄFVERI
Barnhusgatan 3
SE-11123 Stockholm
T + 46 8 20 71 90
www.interior.boraswafveri.se

CARL MALMSTEN
Strandvagen 5B
S-11451 Stockholm
T + 46 8 23 33 80
www.malmsten.se

SOURCES

CBI DESIGN
Repslagargatan 17B
SE-11846 Stockholm
T + 46 8 611 5252
www@cbidesign.se

DAVID-ANDERSEN
Karl Johansgate 20
N-0159 Oslo
T + 47 2 241 6955
www.david-andersen.no

DAVID DESIGN
Nybrogatan 7
SE-11434 Stockholm
T + 46 8 611 9155
www.david.se

DESIGNER'S EYE
Björnekullavägen 265 /11
SE-29194 Kristianstad
T + 46 447 3095
www.designerseye.se

EUKLIDES 20TH CENTURY DESIGN
Pilestredet 75C
N-0354 Oslo
T + 47 3 333 3106
www.euklides.no

FIGGJO
N-4332 Figgjo
T + 47 5 168 3534
www.figgjo.no

FILIPPA & CO
51 Kinnerton Street
London SW1X 8ED
T + 44 20 7245 9160
www.filippaandco.co.uk

FLIN FLON
138 St John Street
London EC1V 4UA
T + 44 20 7253 8849
www.flinflon.co.uk

FREDERICIA FURNITURE
Treldevej 183
DK-7000 Fredericia
T + 45 7 592 3344
www.fredericia.com

FRITZ HANSEN
Allerødvej 9
DK-3450 Allerød
T + 45 4 817 2300
www.fritzhansen.com

GALLERI CHARLOTTE LUND
Skeppargatan 70
SE-11459 Stockholm
T + 46 8 663 0979
www.gallericharlottelund.com

GALLERI STOLEN
Spårvagnshallarna
Birger Jarlsgatan 57
SE-11356 Stockholm
T + 46 8 442 9150
info@galleristolen.se

GEORG JENSEN
Amagertorv 4
DK-1160 Copenhagen
T + 45 3 311 4080
www.georgjensen.com

GUSTAVSBERG
Odelbergsväg 1
SE-13440 Gustavsberg
T + 46 8 57 03 56 63
www.hpfigustavsberg.se

HACKMAN
Hämmeentie 135
FIN-00560 Helsinki
T + 358 204 3911
www.hackmangroup.fi

HADELAND
N-3520 Jevnaker
T + 47 6 131 6400
www.hadeland-glassverk.no

HOLMEGAARD
Amagertorv 6
DK-1160 Copenhagen
T + 45 3 312 4477
www.holmegaard.com

IITTALA
FIN-14500 Iittala
T + 358 204 3915
www.iittala.com

JACKSONS
Sibyllegatan 53
SE-11443 Stockholm
T + 46 8 665 3350
www.jacksons.se

JOBS HANDTRYCK
Västanvik 201
SE-79392 Leksand
T + 46 2 471 2222
www.jobshandtryck.se

KASTHALL
Sibyllegatan 39
SE-11456 Stockholm
T + 46 8 762 8446
www.kasthall.se

KÄLLEMO
PO Box 605
SE-11452 Värnamo
T + 46 3 701 5000
www.kallemo.se

KINNASAND
Lyddevägen 17
SE-51123 Kinna
T + 46 3 203 0300
www.kinnasand.se

KINNASAND UK
13 New North Street
London WC1N 3PJ
T + 46 20 7420 5913
www.kinnasand.com

KIRSUBERJATRÉD
Vesturgata 4
IS-101 Reykjavík
T + 354 562 8990
www.kirs.is

KLARA
Nytorgsgatan 36
SE-10061 Stockholm
T + 46 8 694 9240
www.klara-cbi.se

KLÄSSBOLS
Damastvägen 5
SE-67195 Klässbol
T + 46 5 70 46 01 85
www.klassbols-linne.se

KOSTA BODA
SE-36052 Kosta
T + 46 4 783 4500
www.kostaboda.se

LAMMHULTS MÖBEL
PO Box 26
SE-36030 Lammhult
T + 46 4 72 26 95 00
www.lammhults.se

LE KLINT
Egestubben 13-15
DK-5270 Odense
T + 45 6 618 1920
www.leklint.com

LOUIS POULSEN
Nyhavn 11
DK-1001 Copenhagen
T + 45 3 314 1414
www.louispoulsen.com

MARIMEKKO
Puusepänkatu 4
FIN-0800 Helsinki
T + 358 97 58 71
www.marimekko.fi

MODERNITY
Sibyllegatan 6
Ostermalmstorg
SE-14442 Stockholm
T + 46 8 20 80 25
www.modernity.se

185

CHRONOLOGY

NORDISKA GALLERIET
Nybrogatan 11
SE-11434 Stockholm
T + 46 8 442 8360
www.nordiskagalleriet.com

NORWAY SAYS DESIGN SHOP
Thorvald Meyers gate 15
N-0555 Oslo
T + 47 2 238 2575
www.norwaysays.com

ORREFORS
SE-38040 Orrefors
T + 46 4 813 4000
www.orrefors.se

PORSGRUND
PO Box 100
N-3907 Porsgrunn
T + 47 3 555 0040
www.porsgrund.com

ROSENDAHL
Maglebjergvej 4
DK-2800 Lyngby
T + 45 4 588 6633
www.rosendahl.dk

ROBERT TANDBERG
Dronningensgate 8A
N-0152 Oslo
T + 47 2 247 3020
www.roberttandberg.no

R.O.O.M.
Alströmergatan 20
SE-10028 Stockholm
T + 46 8 692 5082
www.room.se

RÖRSTRAND
Box 903
Fiskaregatan 4
SE-53119 Lidköping
T + 46 5 108 2300
www.rorstrand.com

ROYAL COPENHAGEN
Smallegade 47
DK-2000 Fredriksberg
T + 45 3 814 9297
www.royalcopenhagen.com

SKANDIUM
72 Wigmore Street
London W1U 2SG
T + 44 20 7935 2077
www.skandium.com

SKULTUNA
Box 103
SE-73050 Skultuna
T + 46 2 17 83 00
www.skultuna.com

SNOWCRASH
Textilvägen 1
SE-12030 Stockholm
T + 46 8 442 9810
www.snowcrash.se

STELTON
Gammel Vartov Vej 1
DK-2900 Hellerup
T + 45 3 962 3055
www.stelton.dk

SVENSKT TENN
Strandvägen 5
SE-11484 Stockholm
T + 46 8 670 1600
www.svenskttenn.se

SWEDESE
PO Box 156
SE-56723 Vaggeryd
T + 46 3 937 9702
www.swedese.se

VESSEL
114 Kensington Park Road
London W11 2PW
T + 44 20 7727 8001
www.vesselstore.com

1654 The *Karolinsk* period commences with the reign of Karl X Gustav

1726 Rörstrand established in Sweden

1742 Kosta glassworks established in Sweden

1762 Hadeland glassworks established in Norway

1760 The Gustavian style begins taking shape some 11 years before Gustav III ascends the Swedish throne

1775 Royal Copenhagen porcelain workshop established in Denmark

1790 The neoclassical style spreads to Scandinavia

1809 Sweden cedes Finland to Russia; Finland becomes a Russian Grand Duchy

1810 French Empire style initiates the 'Swedish Empire' style

1814 Norway is ceded to Sweden by Denmark

1825 Gustavsberg kilns established in Sweden

1825 Holmegaard glassworks established in Denmark

1872 Fritz Hansen established in Denmark

1873 Arabia kilns established in Finland

1876 David-Andersen goldsmithery established in Norway

1880 'Dragon' style takes hold in Norway

1881 Iittala glassworks founded in Finland

1886 Porsgrund kilns established in Norway

1898 Orrefors established in Sweden

1899 Carl Larsson publishes *Ett Hem* in Sweden

1901 National Romantic movement takes hold in Sweden and Finland

1904 Georg Jensen silversmithery established in Copenhagen

1905 Norway gains independence from Sweden

1916 Carl Malmsten establishes his studio in Stockholm

1920 Nordic Classicism takes hold in Sweden

1924 Svenskt Tenn established in Stockholm

1924 Kaare Klint designs first functionalistic furniture

1930 Functionalism debuts at the Stockholm Exhibition

1935 Artek established by Alvar and Aino Aalto in Helsinki

1937 Josef Frank acknowledged as leading proponent of 'Swedish Modern' at the World's Fair in Paris

1943 Le Klint established in Denmark

1951 Marimekko established in Finland

1968 Villa Spies built in Sweden

1970 *10-gruppen* established in Stockholm

1976 Sweden's *Svenska Slöjdföreningen* reinvents itself as Svensk Form

1976 Now under the direction of the Åfors Group, Kosta is renamed Kosta Boda

1983 Arabia take over Rörstrand, then taken over by Hackman who also acquire Iittala

1990 Orrefors merges with Kosta Boda

1990 Thomas Sandell founds design and architecture practice in Stockholm

1991 Snøhetta architects established in Oslo

1993 Claesson Koivisto Rune design and architect practice established in Stockholm

1997 Royal Scandinavian take over Orrefors Kosta Boda

1998 Snowcrash established in Helsinki

1999 Norway Says established in Oslo

2001 IKEA introduce the *Bo Klok* 'Smarter Living' concept

2002 Bertil Vallien's glass altarpiece installed in Växjö cathedral

INDEX

ACKNOWLEDGEMENTS

PICTURE CREDITS

The publisher would like to thank the following photographers, agencies and organizations for their kind permission to reproduce the photographs in this book.

6 Åke E:son Lindman (Architects: Cecilia and Per Margen-Wigow); 12–13 Jiri Havran/Villa Stenersen, Oslo (Designer: Arne Korsmo); 14–5 Elizabeth Whiting and Associates; 16 Ingalill Snitt; 19 Mats Landin/Nordiska Museet; 22 Lars Hallén/Design Press; 25 Lars Hallén/Design Press (Architect: Eliel Saarinen); 26 Lennart Olson/Swedish Society of Crafts and Design (Interior Designer: Thea Leonhard); 28–29 Staffan Berglund; 36 Ingalill Snitt; 37 Elizabeth Whiting and Associates; 45 Elizabeth Whiting and Associates; 54 Nationalmuseum, Stockholm/Bridgeman Art Library; 55 Richard Bryant/Arcaid; 58 Arkitekturmuseet, Stockholm; 59 Lars Hallén/Design Press (Architect: Gunnar Asplund); 64 Swedish Society of Crafts and Design (Designer: Nisse Strinning); 65 Karl Erik Granath/Nordiska Museet; 70 Lena Köller/Skarp; 71 Paul Ryan/International Interiors (Designer: Mathias Wagmö); 75 below Paul Ryan/International Interiors (Architect: Olle Rex); 80 left Kim Ahm/House of Pictures (Stylist: Andrea Grunnet-Jensen/House Of Pictures); 87 Alexander van Berge/Taverne Agency (Stylist: Ulrika Lundgren); 89 Paul Ryan/International Interiors (Designer: Mathias Wagmö); 90 Jan Baldwin/Narratives (Owner: Richard and Helen Somogyvari); 110 and 111 left Åke E:son Lindman (Architects: Cecilia and Per Margen-Wigow); 111 right Stellan Herner (Architect: Thomas Sandell and Stylist: Gill Renlund); 112–113 Mirjam Bleeker/Taverne Agency (Stylist: Frank Visser); 114 left Åke E:son Lindman (Architects: Cecilia and Per Margen-Wigow); 114 right Kim Ahm/House of Pictures (Stylist: Andrea Grunnet-Jensen); 120 Ray Main/Mainstream (Designer: Nanna Ditzel); 126 Alexander van Berge/Taverne Agency (Stylist: Ulrika Lundgren); 136 Ray Main/Mainstream; 137 Ray Main/Mainstream (Designer: Nanna Ditzel); 138 Jan Baldwin/Narratives (Owner: Richard and Helen Somogyvari); 140 left V&A Picture Library (Designer: Eero Aarnio); 140 right Ray Main/Mainstream; 141 Karl Erik Granath/Nordiska Museet; 144 Chris Harrison/Bleed AS (Designer: Norway Says); 145 Kim Ahm/House of Pictures (Stylist: Pil Bredahl); 168 left Nordiska Museet; 168 centre and right Birgit Brnvall/Nordiska Museet; 175 Marimekko Corporation; 176 left Lena Köller/Skarp.

Every effort has been made to trace the copyright holders and we apologize in advance for any unintentional omissions, and would be pleased to insert the appropriate acknowledgement in any subsequent publication.

SPECIAL PHOTOGRAPHY CREDITS

Endpapers 'Nakki' textile by Sari Sylväluoma for Liminal; 1 location Chrystina CNG Schmidt and Magnus England, owners of Skandium; 2 table and bowl by Tapio Wirkkala, location Andrew Duncanson, owner of Modernity; p 4–5 location Jacksons, Stockholm, left to right 'Apple Vase' by Ingeborg Lundin for Orrefors, 'Tulip Glasses' by Nils Landberg for Orrefors, 'Kremlin Bells' by Kaj Franck for Nuutajärvi, 'Singing Bird' by Timo Sarpaneva for Kosta, vase by Vicke Lindstrand for Kosta; 7 location and interior designer Filippa Naess; 10, back cover and 31 location Lars Nittve, architect Shideh Shaygan of Shaygan Interior Architecture; 34 location and interior designer Filippa Naess; 35, 39, 40 right, 43, 44 and 46 location Skansen, open-air museum, Sweden; 47 location Filippa & Co; 50–51 location and interior designer Filippa Naess; 66–67 location and interior designer Henri Davies, Tyger Design, ceramics from the Warm Range by Tonfisk; 68 location Lena and Hans Blomberg, architects Gunnar Orefelt, Carla Garbagni and Anna Nyström Davis for Orefelt Associates Ltd; 69 location and interior designer Henri Davies, Tyger Design; 72 left and centre location Ted Hesselbom and Peppe Bergström; 74 architect Thomas Sandell; 75 top and 81 location Lena and Hans Blomberg, architects Gunnar Orefelt, Carla Garbagni and Anna Nyström Davis for Orefelt Associates Ltd; 76 location and interior designer Henri Davies, Tyger Design; 78 location Hotel Birger Jarl, Tulegatan 8, SE-104 32 Stockholm, T + 46 8 674 1800, www.birgerjarl.se, room by Thomas Sandell; 79 location Lars Nittve, architect Shideh Shaygan of Shaygan Interior Architecture; 82–84 architect Thomas Sandell; 85 location Jacksons, Stockholm; 86 left location and interior designer Henri Davies, Tyger Design; 86 right location Svenskt Tenn, Stockholm; 88 location Chrystina CNG Schmidt and Magnus England, owners of Skandium; 91 location Lars Nittve, architect Shideh Shaygan of Shaygan Interior Architecture, painting by Torsten Andersson, sculpture by Truls Melin, sculpture on table by Yinka Shinibare; 92 location Jacksons, Stockholm; 94 location Lars Nittve, architect Shideh Shaygan of Shaygan Interior Architecture, photograph on wall artist Maria Friberg © DACS 2003; 95 location Lars Nittve, architect Shideh Shaygan of Shaygan Interior Architecture; 97 right Svenskt Tenn, Stockholm; 100–102 location Lena and Hans Blomberg, architects Gunnar Orefelt, Carla Garbagni and Anna Nyström Davis for Orefelt Associates Ltd; 105 top left location Andrew Duncanson, owner of Modernity; 105 bottom left location Jacksons, Stockholm; 105 bottom right location Lars Nittve, architect Shideh Shaygan of Shaygan Interior Architecture; 106–107 location Chrystina CNG Schmidt and Magnus England, owners of Skandium; 109 location Hotel Birger Jarl, Tulegatan 8, SE-104 32 Stockholm, T + 46 8 674 1800, www.birgerjarl.se, room by Johanna Kohlin and Agenta Petterson; 115 location Peter and Gunilla Eneroth, architect Marjatta Brummer; 116–117 sofa, chair and foot stool by Carl Malmsten, 118 location Svenskt Tenn, Stockholm; 119 location Peter and Gunilla Eneroth, architect Marjatta Brummer; 121 location and interior designer Henri Davies, Tyger Design; 123 top left and bottom right location and interior designer Henri Davies, Tyger Design; 123 top right location Ted Hesselbom and Peppe Bergström; 123 bottom left location Andrew Duncanson, owner of Modernity; 127 location and interior designer Henri Davies, Tyger Design; 128–129 location Ted Hesselbom and Peppe Bergström; 131 location Andrew Duncanson, owner of Modernity, painting by Alexus Hüber; 132–133 location Chrystina CNG Schmidt and Magnus England, owners of Skandium; 139 location Jacksons, Stockholm; 142 location Andrew Duncanson, owner of Modernity; 146–147 location Jacksons, Stockholm, ceramics by Wilhem Kåge for Gustavsberg; 148 location Svenskt Tenn, Stockholm; 150 location Andrew Duncanson, owner of Modernity, 151 top location Lena and Hans Blomberg; 151 bottom location Jacksons, Stockholm; 152 location Jacksons, Stockholm; 153 location Andrew Duncanson, owner of Modernity; 155 location Chrystina CNG Schmidt and Magnus England, owners of Skandium; 156 top left location Jacksons, Stockholm; 156 top right location Peter and Gunilla Eneroth; 158 and 161 location Ted Hesselbom and Peppe Bergström; 163 location Jacksons, Stockholm; 164 left location Chrystina CNG Schmidt and Magnus England, owners of Skandium; 164 centre location Ted Hesselbom and Peppe Bergström; 164 right location Jacksons, Stockholm; 172 location Lena and Hans Blomberg, architects Gunnar Orefelt, Carla Garbagni and Anna Nyström Davis for Orefelt Associates Ltd; 174 location Chrystina CNG Schmidt and Magnus England, owners of Skandium; 177 location and interior designer Henri Davies, Tyger Design.

The publisher and author would like to thank the following stores and designers for their kind loan of furniture and accessories for photography.

Bo!
Östgötagatan 2, SE-116 25, Stockholm
T + 46 8 643 69 14

Designor AB
Norrlandsgatan 18, SE-111 43, Stockholm
T + 46 8 678 07 75

Eat My Handbag Bitch Gallery
37 Drury Lane, London WC2B 5RR
T + 44 20 7836 0830
www.eatmyhandbagbitch.co.uk

Georg Jensen
15 New Bond Street, London W1S 3ST
T + 44 20 7499 6541
www.georgjensen.com

Georg Jensen & Royal Scandinavia
Birger Jarlsgatan 13, SE-111 45 Stockholm
T + 46 8 545 040 80
www.georgjensen.com

Iittala-butiken
Norrlandsgatan 18, SE-111 43 Stockholm
T + 46 8 678 07 05
www.kasthall.se

Kasthall
Sibyllegatan 39, SE-114 42 Stockholm
T + 46 8 662 27 11
www.kasthall.se

Oggetti
143 Fulham Road, London SW3 6SD
T + 44 20 7584 9808

Ordning & Reda
21–22 New Row, London WC2N 4LE
T + 44 20 7240 8090
www.ordning-reda.com

SCP
135–139 Curtain Road, London EC2A 3BX
T + 44 20 7739 1869
www.scp.co.uk

Themes & Variations
231 Westbourne Grove, London W11 2SE
T + 44 20 7727 5531
www.themesandvariations.com

Thanks also to the following, whose contact details can be found in the Directory: Asplund, Boda Nova-Höganäs Keramik, Carl Malmsten (p 185), Liminal (p 183), Designer's Eye, Fritz Hansen, Jacksons (p 185), Modernity, Nordiska Galleriet (p 186), Skandium, Svenstk Tenn and Vessel (p 186).

On the map:

GREENLAND

ICELAND
• Thingvellir
Reykjavík

FINNMARK

RUSSIA

Norwegian Sea

FINLAND
• Jyväskylä

Faroe Islands
(Denmark)

Atlantic Ocean

• Trondheim   • Östersund

• Ålesund

NORWAY
• Mora
• Bergen   • Falun
                 DALARNA

• Nuutajärvi
• Turku   ◉ Helsinki

◉ Oslo
• Porsgrunn   ◉ Stockholm   ESTONIA

• Stavanger
                 SWEDEN
Kristiansand•   Visby•

Gothenburg• • Borås   GOTLAND Sea   LATVIA
              SMÅLAND
• Ålborg
Århus•   Helsingborg   • Orrefors
DENMARK   SKÅNE   LITHUANIA
Copenhagen◉   *Baltic Sea*
• Malmö
Fredericia•   Falsterbo   KALININGRAD
                                        (Russia)

North Sea

UNITED
KINGDOM   BELARUS

IRELAND   POLAND

0   200   400   600km   GERMANY

AUTHOR'S ACKNOWLEDGEMENTS

This book was a pleasure to research and write. This project was realized through the support of many people, and I thank all of them for giving generously of their time and knowledge. It has been a privilege to work with such a fantastic team: Muna Reyal, who commissioned the project; Alexander Crispin, whose spectacular photography took us far beyond our initial vision for the book; Zia Mattocks, who was a source of inspiration as well as an excellent editor; Liz Boyd and Sarah Hopper for sourcing the perfect archive images; Alison Wormleighton, who edited the manuscript with insight and enthusiasm. I would especially like to thank Megan Smith, whose outstanding art direction and book design gave beautiful expression to all our hard work.

At home in London, I appreciated the support of Anne-Lise Kjaer, Filippa Naess, Caroline van Luthje, Trine Ulrich, Mette Baklund, Gunnar Orefelt, Henri Davies, Renee Kopal, Anne-Katrine Dolven, Evelyna Ruhnbro, Marianna Wahlsten, Kerstin Ever and Gunilla Nordquist. Special thanks to Mats and Agneta Bergqvist, Maria Schottenius at the Embassy of Sweden, Nils Martin Gunneng at the Royal Norwegian Embassy and Pirjo Pellinen at the Embassy of Finland.

In Sweden, I was hosted by the Swedish Institute and given private access to the archives and collections of the Nordiska Museet, the National-museum and Skansen, a special privilege which I appreciated and enjoyed. I would also like to thank Ewa Kumlin, Markus Sterky, Mårten Claesson, Gunilla Kinn, Bo Madestrand, Maria Friberg, Lena Bergström, Shideh Shaygan, Lars Nittve, Åsa Jobs, Peter and Gunilla Eneroth, Niklas and Monika Midby, Carl and Eva Lewenhaupt, Lena Larsson Blomberg, Ted Hesselbom, Patric Malteus, Per and Anita Wästberg, Anders Wall, Yvonne Sörensen, Thomas Sandell, Lars Sjöberg, Staffan Carlén, Paul Jackson, Inge Svensson, Sophie Giescke Linné and Karin Lindahl.

My trip to Norway was supported by the Norwegian Ministry of Foreign Affairs for which I thank Kristine Hauer Århus. I appreciated the inspiration of Andreas Engesvik, Craig Dykers, Kjetil Thorsen, Erik Klaveness, Erling Kagge, Sari Syväluoma, Nikolai Handeland, Terje Jacobsen, Bo Wallström, Widar Halén at Kunstindustrimuseet and the guides at the Viking Museum in Oslo. Thanks to Jiri Havran for photographing Villa Stenersen.

My thanks to Marianne Gulløv at Fritz Hansen and Trine Hedegaard at Rosendahl International in Denmark, to Päivi Jantunen and Harri Koskinen in Finland, and to Adalsteinn Ingolfsson and Hrafnkell Birgisson in Iceland.